Bodywork

Bodywork

Primary Children, Dance and Gymnastics

Ann Davies and Val Sabin

STANLEY THORNES

Contents _____

5 Cross-curricular Projects   143

6 Useful Addresses   173

Note to Readers

Primary school resources for dance and gymnastics

This book has been written in response to requests from teachers for resources to enable them to teach dance and gymnastics in primary schools. It is intended to demystify both activities and to give teachers the confidence either to begin to teach, or to develop their existing expertise in both areas.

We look at the similarities and the differences between the two activities and show how the same movement ideas can be used as the starting points for units of work for both dance and gymnastics for each year group in Key Stages 1 and 2. We show how dance and gymnastics can benefit each other and how it is the attitude to movement and the purpose for which it is used that will help to differentiate between the two activities.

For teachers with little or no previous experience of teaching dance and/or gymnastics, the units of work have been written in as much detail as possible so that they can be used immediately, with each teacher adapting the material to suit his/her own teaching styles and individual needs, together with those of the children being taught.

Experienced teachers, on the other hand, will probably use the material in these units as a springboard for their own ideas. All the work in the units has been based on the programmes of study – both general and activity specific – and the end of Key Stage descriptions in the National Curriculum Order for Physical Education.

Finding the appropriate accompaniment for dance often presents difficulties and therefore music for the dance units of work has been composed and accompanies this book.

Teachers often express concern about apparatus work in gymnastics lessons and so a comprehensive section on the organisation, safe-handling and creative ways of setting out and using apparatus has been included.

Having successfully taught some of the units of work and having experienced the challenge, excitement and satisfaction that the teaching of dance and gymnastics can bring, there is more information in Chapter 3 on how to prepare your own material. There is no magic wand that can be waved so that lessons prepare themselves, but there are steps that can be followed to make the process a little easier and these are outlined in this chapter.

Advice is also given on the writing of a school policy for dance and gymnastics and suggested schemes of work for Key Stages 1 and 2, together with a system for assessment, based on National Curriculum requirements, are offered in some detail.

Dance and gymnastics form an essential part of the whole school curriculum and while they are both essential in their own right, they also provide opportunities to reinforce other areas of the curriculum. It is for this reason that cross-curricular links are outlined at the beginning of each unit of work and detailed descriptions of two cross-curricular projects in which dance and gymnastics played a vital role, can be found in Chapter 5.

How to use this book

The order of the contents of this book has been carefully considered so that the reader is taken stage by stage through the principles underlying the successful planning and teaching of dance and gymnastics in the primary school.

Each reader will probably want to use the book differently. If you already have expertise and experience in teaching dance and/or gymnastics, you may wish to turn straight to Chapter 4 where you will find units of work for dance and gymnastics for each year group in Key Stages 1 and 2. Each unit has been covered in depth to include aims, specific objectives for each lesson, suggested corss-curricular links and detailed lesson plans so that you can use them immediately as a basis for your own teaching.

If, however, you do not have experience in teaching dance and gymnastics, you will probably wish to read Chapter 1 first, where the principles underlying the teaching of dance and gymnastics and the particular contribution of dance to a child's artistic and aesthetic education can be found. In this chapter you will also find information on the material and language of movement for both dance and gymnastics in addition to information on dance compostion. You may then wish to read Chapter 4 so that you can use some of the material there to help you to teach some of your own classes. Once you need to generate your own material, Chapter 3 will provide you with help on how to do this.

Some readers may have responsibility for co-ordinating the dance and/or gymnastics programme within their schools. It is for these readers in particular that Chapter 2 has been written. Here you will find sufficient information to help you write a whole school policy for these areas.

Chapter 5 contains detailed descriptions of two cross-curricular projects with the relevant units of work and will hopefully be useful for all readers.

The cassette

Music has been written to accompany most of the dances featured in the book. There is not, however, a musical accompaniment for all dances as it is important that other forms of accompaniment, such as words, sounds and percussion, are explored with pupils. The titles of all the dances used in the book follow with the track number where applicable:

1   Humpty Dumpty

2   Where the Wild Things Are

3   Winnie the Pooh

–   Rain

4   Jack Frost

5   Coming to School

6   Jack-in-the-Box

7   Anger, Sadness, Happiness

–   Cats

–   Snow

8   Funfair Mirrors

9   Oriental Adventure

10   Space Invaders

11   Spaghetti

–   A Fight – Lowry
     (The music used for this dance is the signature tune for BBC television's snooker programme, *Pot Black*. As it is widely, commercially available, it is not included on the cassette.)

12   Landscape

13   Waterless Method of Swimming Instruction

Reflections on the National Curriculum

The statutory Order for Physical Education in the National Curriculum states that at Key Stages 1 and 2 all pupils should pursue specified programmes of study in dance, gymnastic activities and games. In addition, swimming, athletics and outdoor and adventurous activities should also be included at points in Key Stage 2. Swimming may also be included at Key Stage 1.

Reservations have been expressed about the Order: there is only one un-named attainment target, which is the sum of the end of Key Stage descriptions, and in common with the Orders for Art and Music, no levels of attainment have been included. Will there be sufficient guidance for teachers to teach and assess adequately without specified levels of attainment and with only one attainment target? Do the end of Key Stage descriptions demonstrate clear lines of progression in each activity? These are questions which are still to be answered together with the question of how dance will fare now that it is included in the Order for Physical Education, rather than in an arts context.

There are, however, very positive aspects concerning the Order. Nothing in it should hinder the good teaching that is already taking place and it should ensure that eventually all children aged from 4 to 11 years at least have access to a broad and balanced programme of physical activities. Perhaps Physical Education (PE) is not the most natural home for the teaching of dance as an arts activity, but at least it is now a compulsory part of a child's education. The 1988 Education Reform Act made no mention of it whatsoever.

Historically, dance in schools was fostered mainly within PE programmes and the basis of dance is, of course, movement as it is for other PE activities. What distinguishes it, however, from these other activities is its aesthetic and artistic nature when it is taught as an art form. While the inclusion of dance within the PE Order may suggest that it is part of the PE programme, it is of course the responsibility of each school to decide how, when and where it is taught.

It is essential, however, that it is taught sensitively, within an atmosphere that is conducive to creating, imagining, sensing and feeling. The arts are concerned with formulating and clarifying ideas and feelings. They express the creator's ideas and experience of life. This must make the creator, in this case, the pupil, very vulnerable since innermost feelings and thoughts are exposed through the arts and should be treated with care.

Regardless of any changes that may be made to the statutory orders for Physical Education in the Naional Curriculum, every child should child should be entitled to a broad and balanced programme of physical activities taught by effective, imaginative and confident teachers.

We hope that the material in this book will make this possible.

Acknowledgements

We wish to thank colleagues and pupils from the following for their co-operation during the writing of this book:

Abington Vale Middle School
Barton Seagrave Primary School
Helmdon Primary School
Higham Ferrers Junior School
Irchester Junior School
Roade Primary School
Roade Secondary School
Newbottle and Charlton Primary School.

Ann Davies and Val Sabin

copyright acknowledgements

The authors and publishers would like to thank the following for their kind permission to reproduce copyright material: Noel Petty for 'Spaghetti'; HMSO for extracts from *Expressive Arts 5–14: National Curriculum and Assessment in Scotland National Guidelines* (Scottish Office Education Department 1992). Crown copyright is reproduced with the permission of the Controller of HMSO.

The publishers have been unable to trace the copyright holders of 'Cats' by Eleanor Farjeon and 'The Land' by Celia Mayes, and should be grateful for any information regarding either of these.

Photographs by Paul Edwards and Aaron Goddard.

1 First Principles

The importance of dance and gymnastics

To move is to live and without movement there is no life. Through movement human beings have learned to survive. They have developed physical skills of strength, speed and stamina, allowing them to pit their wits against the environment, but they have also used their bodies as outlets for imaginative, creative and expressive impulses and as a means of worship.

In the life of primitive humans, nothing approached the dance in significance. For them it was no mere pastime – it was a sacred activity, at the very root of existence. From birth to sickness and death, initiation, marriage, planting and harvesting, hunting and war – each event had its own dance ritual with its own symbolic meaning.

Movement is just as vital to our survival today. It is an important antidote to the mechanistic and computerised way of life around us. Through participation in physical activities, whether creative or recreative, the pressures of everyday life can be eased.

For children, movement has an additional function; it is a medium for learning about themselves and the world around them and for expressing their feelings and making comments on that world. But above all, children move because of the delight and pleasure it gives them. The satisfaction of learning to ride a bicycle, the thrill of swinging from trees or leaping from a height have their own reward and are enjoyed for their own sake.

An awareness of what the body is doing is made possible by the kinaesthetic sense. The nerve endings in the muscles and joints send messages to the brain to indicate the body's position and the speed and way in which it is moving.

Kinaesthetic awareness is essential to the mastery of movement and this, in turn, is vital to both dance and gymnastics, in which the performer's body is the instrument of the action. Both activities demand a controlled and efficient use of the body through the acquisition of physical skills and the development of mental ability. Both activities aid the development of accurate observational skills leading to discrimination and the making of decisions and judgements. They also contribute to the learning of interpersonal skills – encouraging co-operation, adaptation and sensitivity to other people – and contribute to the child's self-confidence and self-esteem.

The difference between dance and gymnastics

There are obviously many similarities between gymnastics and dance since they both use movement as their starting point and are both concerned with composing, performing and appreciating. Both provide children with opportunities for inventive and creative responses to stimuli and help to develop versatility in a variety of purposeful situations. There is, however, an essential difference between them. Gymnastics is mainly concerned with the development of skilful body management and may be described as objective in purpose, with any expressive qualities being merely incidental. Dance, too, requires skilful body management, but the ultimate concern in dance is with these expressive qualities – with the meaning of movement, rather than its purely practical function, and it is, above all, concerned with the aesthetic and artistic nature of movement. Aesthetic qualities may be perceived in many aspects of Physical Education, especially in gymnastics when movements may be enjoyed for their energy, rhythmic patterns and clarity of line and shape, but it is in dance where they will most often be evident and are deliberately employed, in order to communicate an intended idea.

Aesthetic education

Dance offers a context for aesthetic education, giving pupils opportunities to experience life aesthetically, that is 'to sense the drama in every moment of life, in the conflict of colours and shapes, sounds and rhythms' (H.S. Broudy, *Enlightened Cherishing*, University of

Illinois Press, 1972). It is concerned with heightening their awareness of the qualities of objects and events and encouraging the viewing of things purely for the way they look, sound or feel, with no ulterior motive, except that of enjoying them for what they are, for their qualities of line, pattern, dynamics, colour, texture and shape. This viewing, however, cannot be passive. Instead, we need to give it the sort of attention that makes us sit on the edge of our seats in order to become aware of all the subtle and complex details of the objects or activities.

This, however, requires cultivation, since the practical pursuits of everyday life tend to make us less sensitive to the objects or activities that may cause aesthetic experiences. As teachers, we should be trying to ensure that this sensitivity is not lost, but is nurtured and developed by drawing children's attention to the sensory, formal, temporal and expressive qualities of objects and events and by encouraging children to respond imaginatively to them.

If children are looking at an object, whether natural or machine-made, the first aspect of it that they will probably notice will be its sensory properties. Is it smooth, hard, delicate, cold or sharp? These qualities are essential to the object or artefact and to change any of them would be to change the experience had while looking at the object. The feelings aroused when looking at a marble sculpture will be very different from those felt when looking at one made of welded machine parts.

Equally important are the formal and expressive properties of the object. The form refers to its compstition and design, with its rhythm, variations, highlights and contrasts, while the expressive properties spring from the giving of form to a sensory content. Through the arrangement of the materials used for the object, the perceiver's imagination is stirred and the meaning of the object is realised. Obviously, when looking at activities or events such as dance, temporal qualities, such as the languorous or urgent nature of the movement, will also be vital to its expressive nature and, therefore, to the aesthetic experience.

Children should be encouraged to make informed judgements about and respond to aesthetic qualities. These judgements, however, should be justified through direct reference to something in the object or activity which everyone can perceive, so that it is not enough to say, 'I like it' or 'I don't like it'.

Aesthetic qualities are embodied in many aspects of dance. They will be seen in traditional and folk dances. While these are obviously enjoyed by the dancers themselves for social and kinaesthetic reasons, they are also enjoyed and appreciated by onlookers for their intricacy of pattern, rhythm, line and form. But it is only when dance is taught as an artistic activity that aesthetic elements are deliberately used 'to enhance the experience for both performer and audience, to create meaning and communicate through movement' (*Dance in Schools*, Arts Council of Great Britian, 1993).

The contribution of dance to artistic education

For dance to be taught as an artistic activity, three areas must be addressed, those of composition, performance and appreciation. **Composition** entails creating dances with movements being intentionally selected, refined, moulded, shaped and formed into an identifiable whole to communicate an intended idea. The composition is a conscious expression of the composer's comment on the world. The dance only seeks to portray these comments, emotions or ideas and the performer does not have to 'feel' what the dance reflects. The composer will have abstracted the essence from actual feeling or literal movement, which can then be modified and manipulated to be used as a symbol to convey meaning. Therefore, in the dance based on the emotions of anger, sadness and happiness described on pages 81–4 the children were not asked to be angry, but they were encouraged to talk about their observations of what people sometimes did when they felt these emotions. They suggested that stamping, jumping up and down and shaking fists conveyed anger. They also noticed the strength of these movements. They observed that when people were sad they tended to sink down, closing their arms and legs into the body, with the strength evaporating, while when they were happy, their movements tended to rise with an outward focus and light quality. These movements were then exaggerated by the children and made into movement phrases or motifs. These were then repeated exactly, or varied by using different body parts, levels or by making the movement travel instead of remaining on the spot. The ideas were then refined and shaped, emphasising highlights and contrasts to give form to the dance.

While composition entails the making of dances, **performance** is concerned with dancing – with the interpretation or recreation of the compostion.

To do this successfully the performer must have physical skills, an understanding of the composer's intention and a sensitivity to the accompaniment, other performers and the space in which the dance is to be performed. The dancers will also need to develop skills of projection and interpretative and expressive qualities so that they can successfully convey the composer's idea.

This does not mean that the pupils need to stand in lines doing exercises, which are often irrelevant and unconnected to the dance idea. Instead, they should be encouraged to develop a flexible, strong body and to move with fluency through the exploration of movement possibilities suggested by the dance idea. Pupils should be aware of their own physical limitations and should be encouraged to work to improve their technical skills, but an over-emphasis on technique can restrict creative abilities, resulting in an over-reliance on the teacher and sterile ideas.

Performance in a learning context does not

necessarily mean a full-blown dance performance in a theatre. This may sometimes be relevant, but usually performance means sharing in a class situation. It may begin with a partner, when the children evaluate each other's work and offer constructive comments for its improvement. It may then progress to sharing with the rest of the class and then perhaps with another class or the rest of the school in an assembly. Obviously, there will be times when it is appropriate to show the work to parents or a wider audience. This may mean a great deal of time is spent on 'polishing' the performance, which can be very time-consuming and of questionable educational value. If, however, it is an integral part of the whole process of dance education, it can be a very worthwhile experience for performers and audience alike.

Looking at dances provides endless opportunities to develop the pupil's skills of **appreciation**. Through guided questioning the children can be encouraged to describe and interpret what they have seen, in terms of the performance and composition of the dance. They should also be encouraged to make value judgements concerning the dances and be helped to substantiate their opinions with specific reference to what actually exists within the dance and how well it was performed. In addition to this objective evaluation, children must also be allowed to say how the dance makes them 'feel' since education in the arts should encourage the education of feeling and, therefore, children should be encouraged to articulate these feelings.

Often the role of critic is associated with sitting down for long periods of time to contemplate the dance. It is sometimes divorced from the making and performing roles. These roles, however, are not distinct from one another, since there is much that is creative in the interpretation of a work in performance. There is also, inevitably, a creative element in the insight and imagination required of the critic, just as these two latter qualities are applicable to the making and performing roles, while judgements as to suitability and appropriateness pervade all three roles.

In addition to watching dances or parts of dances performed by their peers, children should also have access to dances performed by professional artistes or companies.

The literature of dance

Access to the 'literature' of any art form is invaluable in the understanding of that particular art and dance is no exception in this respect. In order to create dances, good models must be available for the pupils to view. Just as it would be inconceivable to think of a fine art course that did not include access to established two-dimensional and three-dimensional art works, or a music course that did not encourage pupils to listen to pieces by established composers, similarly studying dance without reference to existing repertoire would be equally unsatisfactory. The appreciation of repertoire can be used as the basis for composition, through the identification of the formal aspects of the dance. Motifs used in the dance can be developed and varied by pupils as a starting point for their own compositions, or the dynamic or spatial aspects of the dance can inspire the pupils to create a dance on similar, but not identical lines, as shown in Chapter 4 when a video recording of Waterless Method of Swimming Instruction was used in this way. Parts of the dance can also be learned by the pupils to improve their performance skills. How much easier it is to dance expressively and fluently with the image of a 'good' performance in one's mind. Even the most highly trained dance teacher would find it impossible to dance equally well in every dance style or to match the different technical and interpretative skills of Nureyev, Fonteyn, Bannerman and Tharp. Use of repertoire, either live or on film or video makes it possible for pupils to have access to these models, thus giving them the opportunity to improve their own performance skills.

The use of repertoire can also give pupils access to a rich diversity of cultural forms. Dance epitomises the expression of culture and heritage and can provide a focus for both multi-cultural and dance education. It is important, however, that pupils are not offered a diluted or westernised version of what is purported to be the authentic dance of another culture. Instead, pupils should see the real thing, either on video or in live performance, and be taught by dance artists with a deep knowledge, understanding, technical expertise and respect for that particular dance form.

The teacher's role in the use of video recordings or in theatre visits to see dances, or in visits by dance artists and companies to the school, is vital. Since dance is so transient, then the pupils will need to be very well prepared for what they are going to see, in order to derive maximum benefit from it. Obviously, video recordings can be stopped for specific points to be emphasised or made, but, of course, this is not possible in live performances. Background about the company performing the work and certainly about the choreographer, including descriptions of some of his/her works, may help to put the specific work in context. Some analysis as an aid to better perception may help before the performance and, possibly, again after it, so that the pupils will be aware of the sensory, temporal, formal and, therefore, expressive qualities of the piece, enabling them to have some cues and signposts to help them. It may be possible for the teacher, or a dancer from the company, to teach a part of the dance to the pupils before the performance, since this really fixes the roving eye on what there is to be sensed. Much information abut dance works can be obtained from books and programmes showing photographs of the dance work, thus enabling the teacher to discuss details of lighting, costume, props and set and their significance in the dance, again drawing pupils' attention to the sensory qualities of the piece, all for the purpose of better perception.

The value of dance artists in education obviously extends further than the known works they may bring with them. Smaller companies and individual artists will usually perform works that neither the teacher nor the pupils will have seen, so that it may be the artists themselves who prepare the children for what they are going to see – perhaps during workshops with the children, or lecture demonstrations, or by explaining a little about the performance immediately before it and by taking questions after it.

The value of such an artist could be seen in a week's residency by Rosamund Shreeves in a Northamptonshire middle school. Rosamund's own one-woman performance was entitled 'Ocean' and each class in the school had been working on this topic for approximately a month before the residency. Aspects of the performance and the project included pollution, objects that might be found on a beach, undersea creatures and the many moods of the ocean. Because of the work already done in the school and because of Rosamund's incredibly effective setting of the scene and mood, through explanation, lighting and sound, the effect of her performance on the children was stunning. The extent to which the children had been involved and completely captured by the quality of movement and the moods evoked became increasingly apparent during the workshops throughout the week. The children had perceived far more than had been expected and this was shown in the quality of their own movement, often incorporating elements of Rosamund's performance, but integrated into their own way of moving and this happened before Rosamund had a chance to teach them again.

During her performance and the residency, Rosamund paid great attention to the use of props and the subtle details of them. She had made sleeves in the shape of fish, with iridescent scales and markings, and drew the children's attention to, and encouraged their perception of, the nuances and range of colour, pattern, shape and form of the fish. Partly through their discussion of the movement qualities of the fish and through Rosamund's own performance wearing the sleeves, it was obvious when the children made and wore their own sleeves, that the aesthetic images Rosamund had helped to create for them existed in reality for many of the children and this could be seen in the quality of their movements and in their own dance compositions.

Rosamund Shreeves's residency epitomised the value of bringing live dance performances into schools – it gave both teachers and children access to 'good' models of dance in terms of both composition and performance. It stimulated numerous new dance ideas and allowed critical appraisal to take place, but above all it provided untold opportunities for everyone to experience dance aesthetically with the firing of the imagination which that brings. No amount of swamping children with works of art can ensure that these will

bring about aesthetic experiences, but what can be done is to provide opportunities for these experiences to occur. By creating and capturing a mood and encouraging children's attention to detail and by encouraging them to perceive the sensory, formal, temporal and expressive qualities of her dances, Rosamund brought the magic of dance to all those who saw her.

The material and language of movement

Movement is not always gymnastics or dance, but gymnastics and dance always involve movement, with movement being the raw material for both activities. In order to use movement to create dances and gymnastic sequences children need to know, understand and be able to use a movement vocabulary just as they use words and numbers to solve problems in other areas of the curriculum.

There are many ways of looking at and describing movement, but we have found the analysis of movement based on Rudolf Laban's principles to be particularly useful. Whenever human movement occurs, the body does *something, somewhere, somehow* and possibly in relation to *someone* or *something*.

Let us look at these aspects in more detail.

1 The body

Which parts of the body are moving?

In young children it may very well be that the whole of the body is involved in the action, but gradually children become capable of isolating body parts so that the emphasis may be on hands and feet, on moving different joints or surfaces of the body. Attention may be drawn to which body parts lead the movement or which parts support or receive weight.

What actions are taking place?

The body can bend, stretch and twist enabling it to:
- **transfer weight** – e.g. kneel, sit, cartwheel, bunny jump, collapse, fall, rock, sway.
- **travel** – this involves the body moving from one space to another, e.g. running, walking, skipping, slithering, sliding, creeping, rolling, galloping.
- **turn** – this involves the body rotating, e.g. spinning, cartwheeling, rolling, spiralling, somersaulting, pivoting.
- **jump** – this involves the body being suspended in the air, e.g. leaping (from one foot to the other), hopping (from one foot to the same foot), bouncing (from two feet to two feet), jumping (from one foot to two feet or from two feet to one foot). It is also possible to jump using other parts of the body, e.g.

hands to feet, feet to hands, knees to feet, head and hands to feet.

- **gesture** – any movement which does not involve transference of weight, e.g. beckoning, shrugging shoulders, clapping, tilting, stretching and curling, rising and sinking, opening and closing the whole body or body parts.
- **move symmetrically** – this involves both sides of the body doing the same thing at the same time, e.g. bouncing.
- **move asymmetrically** – this involves each side of the body doing something different at the same time, e.g. running, leaping.
- **make different shapes** – e.g. curled, stretched, twisted, flat, tall, thin, curved, arched, pointed, knobbly, symmetric and asymmetric.

The body can also stop moving to **freeze** or **balance** or **pause**.

Many of these categories overlap, for example, it is impossible to travel, turn or jump without transferring weight. Actions, such as rolling, involve turning and travelling, while leaping involves jumping and travelling.

2 Dynamics

How is the action performed?

The dynamic aspects of the action are concerned with energy, time and continuity and will colour the action:

- **Energy** – this refers to the amount of force used to perform the action. This will vary from a great deal, resulting in a feeling of **strength** and **body tension**, to none at all, resulting in a feeling of **heaviness** and **relaxation**. Heaviness and strength are often confused in movement terms. In fact, they are complete opposites. When a small degree of force is used then the movement may be described as **light**. **Lightness** is a very difficult concept to describe and is more associated with an attitude to energy and may be described as being buoyant, delicate or gentle.

  There is usually an optimum amount of energy or force necessary for the effective and economical performance of an action and this may be described as the quantitative aspect of energy, whereas in dance situations in particular, the qualitative aspect is equally important.

- **Time** – this refers to the speed with which the action is performed and will vary from very **fast** to very **slow**. It also includes **acceleration** and **deceleration**.

  In some actions there is a maximum and a minimum or an optimum speed for the skilful execution of that action.

  In the early years of primary school gymnastics and dance, the tendency is to perform all activities at the same speed – fast! – so it is of prime importance to encourage children to move slowly, not only to add contrast to their movement phrases, but so that

they apply the right amount of speed for the successful execution of the action.

In dance situations time will also be used qualitatively so that the dancer's attitude to time will be more obvious than the dancer's actual speed. Such movements may be described as being sharp, sudden, sustained, staccato or legato or unhurried.

- **Continuity** – this refers to the flow of movement, with free flow and bound flow being the two extremes. **Free flow** gives the impression of an ongoing fluidity of movement – movement that would be hard to stop at any given moment. **Bound flow** is much more restrained in manner, with abrupt breaks and little continuity, i.e. movement that could be stopped at any given point.

3 Space

Where is the action taking place?

The body may use:

- **personal space** – the space immediately surrounding the body.
- **general space** – the space in the rest of the room.
- **levels** – there are three levels at which the body can move: high or towards the ceiling, low or near the floor and medium, which is in between.
- **directions** – the body can move forwards, backwards, sideways, up and down and on different diagonals.
- **size** – movements can be big or small, e.g. a leap or a small bounce, a small tap of the foot or a large stamp.
- **pathways** – these are the designs that the body makes in space as it moves across the floor and through the air. The pathway may be straight or curved or it may zigzag or spiral.

4 Relationships

In relation to whom or what is the action being performed?

The action can be performed in relation to:

- parts of the body, e.g. hands can meet and part; feet can have conversations in movement – one foot stamps several times while the other replies with a light tap.
- a prop or piece of apparatus.
- the teacher.
- a partner or a group.
- one group in relation to another group.

This may involve:

- doing the same, i.e. matching;
- mirroring;
- using a question and answer;
- making contrasting movements;
- meeting and parting;
- avoiding, passing, going around;
- surrounding;
- going under, over, between or through;

- moving in unison (everyone moves at the same time as each other) or in canon (dancers or gymnasts take it in turn to do a movement or movement phrase).

The above activities may be performed using the following **group formations:**

A line

A circle

Solid group formations e.g. a square

A wedge

A crescent

A globe

An irregular group formation

A scattered group formation

Composition

1 Dance

To communicate an idea through dance, not only must the appropriate movement content be chosen, but it must be structured and given form.

In order to do this, the following processes may be used:

a Respond to the stimulus. This might initially be a verbal response or it might be a movement response, leading to improvisation and movement exploration.

b Select and refine appropriate movements to express the idea, e.g. jumping and stamping movements to express anger.

c Create a simple movement phrase or motif using the movements selected, e.g. jumping and stamping may become a phrase of three stamps on the spot, then three stamps while turning followed by running and jumping to finish in an angular, strong shape.

d The phrase/motif may then be developed or varied.

Variation of a motif

Some ways in which a motif can be varied:

a It can be repeated by dancing the phrase exactly the same again.

b The **action** features may be varied by:

  i using the opposite side of the body so that the phrase starts on the right foot instead of the left;

  ii using different parts of the body to do the action so that the three stamps while turning in the original phrase could be performed while spinning or turning on the seat;

  iii adding more actions to the original phrase, e.g. an additional turn could be combined with the final jump in the sequence to make it a turning jump.

c The **dynamics** can be varied by doing the whole or part of the motif:

  i very quickly or very slowly;

  ii with a great deal of energy or with a light quality;

  iii with free flow or with bound flow.

The motif can also be varied by changing the rhythmic pattern.

d The **spatial** features of the motif can be varied by dancing the whole or part of the motif using:

  i different directions, e.g. the travelling part of the original motif could move sideways instead of forwards.

ii different levels. The jump could finish at a medium instead of a high level.

iii a different pathway. Instead of travelling along a straight pathway, a zigzag pathway could be used.

iv different size of movement, e.g. if the travelling steps were large, make them smaller when they are repeated.

e The **relationship** features can be varied by:

i reversing the order of the motif so that the motif becomes a jump, followed by travel, then three stamps while turning and then three stamps on the spot; instead of three stamps on the spot, three stamps while turning, travel and jump, as in the original motif.

ii subtracting an action from the motif, e.g. the travelling part of the sequence could be omitted.

How to structure motifs to make dances

Motifs may be made into dances by using simple musical structures as guiding principles, such as:

1 Binary form (AB): Section A is followed by section B.

2 Ternary form (ABA): Section A is followed by section B, with section A repeated.

3 Rondo form (ABACAD): This provides a chorus and verse framework, with section A as the chorus and sections B, C and D as verses.

Narrative form may also be used. This is not a musical form, but is the gradual unfolding of the dance idea to make a story.

Whatever form is used the dance should have a very clear beginning, middle and end. It should also have the following features:

- climaxes and highlights;
- variation and contrasts;
- smooth transitions between phrases and sections;
- proportion, balance and unity

so that all the pieces or sections fit together well to make a satisfying 'whole', which is the dance.

2 Gymnastics

Although gymnastics is concerned mainly with the development of skilful body management, children can be guided to explore and create different combinations of movements. These movements, joined together in a variety of ways can produce creative sequences.

Children will all be introduced to the same basic skills and principles, but the way in which they are put together and performed in a sequence reveals the understanding and creativity of the individual – in the same way that we all have a similar vocabulary, but our own sentence construction, use of words and delivery are unique to the individual.

Once children have learned a basic 'gymnastic' skill, the principles of movement can be used to enhance and add variety to that movement, e.g. to develop a simple movement, a child could:

a travel into it and out of it in different ways

b change its speed, shape or level

c change the direction or pathway

d vary the dynamics

e perform it with a partner or group.

From this simple breakdown it is evident that a given task of 'compose a sequence showing travel, jump, turn and balance' will produce a very wide range of responses.

It is recognised that children can use these different combinations to compose and create sequences of movement which are appropriate, and flow one into the other, and as they move through the learning process they will be guided to evaluate and appreciate the planning and performing of their peers.

2 A Whole School Policy for Dance and Gymnastics

Although one teacher may have the responsibility for organising and writing a whole school policy for dance and gymnastics, all staff must be consulted and involved in its construction and generally agree to its contents. A document which has been designed and approved by everyone is more likely to be delivered with conviction and will have honestly earned the title 'Whole school policy'.

Writing the policy

Obviously, the writing of a policy document may be approached from many different angles, but we have found one of the most effective and comprehensive structures to be the one outlined below.

Rationale

This should evolve from the overall philosophy of the school as written in the school's prospectus and should consider the place of dance and gymnastics in relation to the overall curriculum. Reasons should be given as to why both activities are included in the curriculum and their specific contributions to a child's education.

The leaflet 'Dance in the School Curriculum' sets out the reasons for dance being included in the school curriculum as follows:

> Dance makes a distinctive contribution to the education of all pupils, in that it uses the most fundamental mode of human expression – movement. Through its use of non-verbal communication pupils are able to participate in a way which differs from any other area of learning. It provides aesthetic and cultural education, opportunities for personal expression and it also introduces students to a wealth of traditional, social and theatrical forms. In a broad and balanced curriculum this important area of human experience should not be neglected. – NDTA, NATFHE, SCODHE, CDET, 1990

You might wish to use this as the basis of your rationale for the inclusion of dance, while the following might provide a rationale for the inclusion of gymnastics. Gymnastics

> educates young people in and through the use and knowledge of the body and its movement. It aims to develop physical competence so that pupils are able to move efficiently, effectively and safely and understand what they are doing. It is essentially a way of learning through action, awareness and observation – *Physical Education for ages 5 to 16*, DES/Welsh Office, 1991

Both dance and gymnastics contribute to the whole curriculum in the following areas:
- artistic and aesthetic education;
- personal and social education;
- health and fitness;
- cross-curricular learning.

In addition, dance also contributes to the child's cultural education.

Aims

Secondly, the aims for dance and gymnastics should be outlined. These have been summarised in the Order for Physical Education which states that a balanced PE programme should enable all children, including those with special needs, to participate in a carefully structured range of activities.

Such a programme aims to give pupils opportunities to :

- develop physical competence and promote physical development
- develop artistic and aesthetic understanding within and through movement
- develop personal qualities such as self-esteem, self-confidence, tolerance and empathy
- extend, refine and become more proficient in a range of psychomotor skills
- experience and appreciate the contribution of physical education and the benefits of

participants in physical activities in school and throughout life

- develop problem solving skills
- develop interpersonal skills
- forge links between the school and its community. – *Physical Education in the National Curriculum. Non Statutory Guidance for Teachers*, Curriculum Council for Wales, 1992

All these aims apply equally to a good dance and gymnastics programme.

Safety

At all times the safety of children is of paramount importance, especially in the planning and delivery of a PE programme. The following 'rules' will help to ensure children's safety:

1 suitable clothing for children (e.g. shorts and T-shirt, leotard, or vest and pants) and for staff (appropriate footwear and clothes which allow freedom of movement) should be worn.
2 Jewellery should be removed and hair tied back.
3 A suitable environment should be provided to include:
   a the removal of unnecessary furniture from the working space;
   b a clean, splinter-free floor so that barefoot work can safely take place;
   c the suitable organisation of apparatus;
   d ease of accessibility to gymnastic apparatus, either housed in a storeroom and/or around the hall to allow for safe and efficient handling.

In addition a school policy for lifting and carrying apparatus should be drawn up, indicating approved methods of handling and constructing apparatus. By everyone adopting and practising the same system of handling apparatus, the knowledge, understanding and expertise of the children will develop, allowing them to manage more complex sets of apparatus as the need arises.

Having considered the place of dance and gymnastics in relation to the whole curriculum, the aims of the programme and the safety factors related to its delivery, then the detailed planning can take place.

Developing schemes of work

1 Undertake an analysis of resources to include staff expertise and available equipment.
2 Undertake a time analysis to establish how much time will be committed to teaching dance and gymnastics across the Key Stage.
3 Allocate time, term by term across each of the years in the Key Stage.
4 Teachers within each Key Stage might then meet to discuss and decide on the teaching/learning objectives for dance and gymnastics for each stage. These should be based on the programmes of study, both general and activity specific, and the end of Key Stage descriptions as detailed in the Order for Physical Education. The objectives should also provide a tool for assessment. The content for a scheme of work for each activity is also implicit within the programmes of study. Suggested outlines for schemes of work for both Key Stage 1 and Key Stage 2 appear on pages 10–13.
5 Identify cross-curricular links. Although primary school teachers are familiar with the fostering of learning through a cross-curricular approach, the implementation of the National Curriculum now makes it a necessity in order to be able to deliver the whole curriculum. Physical education will already have been used by many teachers as a vehicle to facilitate learning in other areas of the curriculum, but now in the core subjects alone there are a number of attainment targets and programmes of study which can be covered through themes and situations encountered in dance and gymnastics lessons.
6 Teachers in each year group will then need to break down the content into more manageable units of work lasting approximately six weeks. Each unit should have its own teaching/learning objectives and the learning activities or content which will contribute to the successful attainment of those objectives. A suggested format for the presentation of dance and gymnastics units of work can be found on pages 20–23.
7 Specific lesson plans will then need to be written either by individual teachers or a group of teachers. While planning is taking place other issues will also need to be considered in order to bring about successful learning outcomes. These can be found on page 14.

Key Stage 1: Learning objectives for dance and gymnastics derived from the programmes of study

Dance objectives which apply to all units	Dance-specific objectives	Cross-curricular theme	Common movement objectives for dance and gym	Gymnastics objectives which apply to all units
To enable the child to:		**Unit 1** _____ Growth	To enable the child to show, use and identify:	To enable the child to:
1 respond to a range of stimuli			1 Whole body actions of travelling and turning	1 carry and position apparatus using the correct technique
2 experience and be guided towards making dances with clear beginnings, middles and ends			2 Taking weight on different body parts 3 Quick and slow movements	2 link movements together both on the floor and using apparatus
3 practise, adapt and improve control of individual actions		**Unit 2** _____ Literature	To enable the child to show, use and identify:	3 Practise, adapt and improve control of individual actions
4 link together a series of movements			1 isolated body parts, e.g. hands and feet, middles and heads	
5 describe movements and dance phrases			2 transference of weight to include rolling 3 directions – forwards, backwards, sideways	
	Unit 3 _____ To enable the child to show use and identify rhythmic patterns of movement	Weather	To enable the child to show use and identify:	
			1 quick and slow movements 2 wide, narrow, curled and spiky body shapes 3 high and low levels 4 linear and curved floor pathways 5 travelling and stopping 6 jumping actions	
		Unit 4 _____ Day and night	To enable the child to show, use and identify:	
			1 more ways of turning 2 acceleration and deceleration	
	Unit 5 _____ To enable the child to explore moods and feelings through spontaneous responses and structured tasks	Ourselves (Toys, moods and feelings)	To enable the child to show, use and identify:	
	To enable the child to show, use and identify gesture		1 more jumping actions 2 curled and angular body shapes 3 dynamics – strong, light and relaxed movements 4 working with a partner	
		Unit 6 _____ Mini-beasts	To enable the child to show, use and identify:	
			1 continuity of movement 2 large and small movements 3 balance	

The end of Key Stage descriptions can be clearly addressed by the above objectives.

'Pupils plan and perform simple skills safely, and show control in linking actions together. They improve their performance through practising their skills, working alone and with a partner. They talk about what they and others have done, and are able to make simple judgements. They recognise and describe the changes that happen to their bodies during exercise.' – Draft National Curriculum Orders for England, 1995

Key Stage 2: Learning objectives for dance and gymnastics derived from programmes of study (Units 1 – 4)

Dance objectives which apply to all units	Dance-specific objectives	Cross-curricular theme (if appropriate)	Common movement objectives for dance and gym	Gymnastics objectives which apply to all units
To enable the child to: 1 respond to a range of stimuli and express feelings, moods and ideas 2 make dances with clear beginnings, middles and ends, involving improvising, exploring, selecting and refining content 3 make and vary movement motifs 4 describe and interpret different elements of a dance		**Unit 1** Seeds and growing (stretching and curling)	To enable the child to show, use and identify: 1 whole body actions of travelling in curled up/stretched out body shapes 2 taking weight on different body parts 3 movement on different levels	To enable the child to: 1 carry and position apparatus using the correct technique 2 link more complex sequence of movements together, both on the floor and using apparatus 3 practise, adapt and improve control of individual actions 4 respond to a variety of tasks alone or with a partner 5 understand and use different speeds, directions, levels and shapes
	Unit 2 To enable the child to show, use and identify legato movements and complex step patterns	Matching and Mirroring	To enable the child to show, use and identify: 1 taking weight on different body parts 2 working on different levels 3 a variety of jumping actions 4 continuity of movement 5 travel, jump, turn and balance 6 working with a partner to show matching and mirroring movements	
		Unit 3 Transport	To enable the child to show use and identify: 1 dynamics – explosive movements and smooth movements 2 acceleration and deceleration 3 controlled transference of body weight 4 linear and curved floor patterns 5 working on different levels	
	Unit 4 To enable the child to show, use and identify legato and staccato movements	Symmetry and Asymmetry	To enable the child to show, use and identify: 1 symmetric and asymmetric shapes and movements 2 transference of body weight 3 movement on different levels 4 strong and light movements 5 working with a partner and in fours, using canon and unison	

The end of Key Stage descriptions can clearly be addressed by the above objectives.

'Pupils find solutions, sometimes responding imaginatively, to the various challenges that they encounter in the different areas of activity. They practise, improve and refine performance, and repeat series of movements they have performed previously, with increasing control and accuracy. They work safely alone, in pairs and in groups, and as members of a team. They make simple judgements about their own and others' performance, and use this information effectively to improve the accuracy, quality and variety of their own performance. They sustain energetic activity over appropriate periods of time, and demonstrate that they understand what is happening to their bodies during exercise.' – Draft National Curriculum Orders for England, 1995

Key Stage 2: Learning objectives for dance and gymnastics derived from programmes of study (Units 5 – 8)

Dance objectives which apply to all units	Dance-specific objectives	Cross-curricular theme	Common movement objectives for dance and gym	Gymnastics objectives which apply to all units
To enable the child to:		**Unit 5** — My body	To enable the child to show, use and identify:	To enable the child to:
1 respond to a range of stimuli and express feelings, moods and ideas			1 parts of the body capable of taking weight in a balance and different combinations of body parts which may be used	1 carry and position apparatus using the correct technique
2 make dances with clear beginnings, middles and ends, involving improvising, exploring, selecting and refining content			2 body tension and quality of movement 3 large and small shapes 4 different relationships of the body to the floor 5 balancing and moving on different levels 6 continuity of movement	2 link more complex sequence of movements together, both on the floor and using apparatus
3 make and vary movement motifs		**Unit 6** — Wheels	To enable the child to show, use and identify:	3 practise, adapt and improve control of individual actions
4 describe and interpret different elements of a dance			1 moving close to the floor and far away from the floor 2 different ways of rolling 3 jumping, landing and moving on different levels 4 moving over, under and around a partner 5 transference of body weight	4 respond to a variety of tasks alone or with a partner 5 understand and use different speeds, directions, levels and shapes
		Unit 7 — Moving around	To enable the child to show, use and identify:	
			1 quick and slow movements 2 a variety of levels 3 straight and curved body shapes on the floor and in the air 4 linear and curved floor patterns 5 contrasting body shape with a partner	
		Unit 8 — Magnets	To enable the child to show, use and identify:	
			1 pushing/pulling/swinging and gripping movements 2 body tension and quality of movement 3 different speeds and levels 4 balancing and moving with a partner	

The end of Key Stage descriptions can clearly be addressed by the above objectives.

'Pupils find solutions, sometimes responding imaginatively, to the various challenges that they encounter in the different areas of activity. They practise, improve and refine performance, and repeat series of movements they have performed previously, with increasing control and accuracy. They work safely alone, in pairs and in groups, and as members of a team. They make simple judgements about their own and others' performance, and use this information effectively to improve the accuracy, quality and variety of their own performance. They sustain energetic activity over appropriate periods of time, and demonstrate that they understand what is happening to their bodies during exercise.'
– Draft National Curriculum Orders for England, 1995

Key Stage 2: Learning objectives for dance and gymnastics derived from programmes of study (Units 9 – 12)

Dance objectives which apply to all units	Dance-specific objectives	Cross-curricular theme	Common movement objectives for dance and gym	Gymnastics objectives which apply to all units
To enable the child to: 1 respond to a range of stimuli and express feelings, moods and ideas 2 make dances with clear beginnings, middles and ends, involving improvising, exploring, selecting and refining content 3 make and vary movement motifs 4 describe and interpret different elements of a dance		**Unit 9** Patterns and Pathways	To enable the child to show, use and identify: 1 turning and twisting 2 different speeds, sizes and levels 3 linear and curving shapes and pathways 4 working with a partner 5 making group shapes and formations	To enable the child to: 1 carry and position apparatus using the correct technique 2 link more complex sequence of movements together, both on the floor and using apparatus 3 practise, adapt and improve control of individual actions 4 respond to a variety of tasks alone or with a partner 5 understand and use different speeds, directions, levels and shapes
		Unit 10 Holes and Barriers	To enable the child to show, use and identify: 1 balancing on different body parts 2 working with a partner and larger groups travelling over/under/around 3 body tension and quality of movement 4 transference of body weight 5 continuity of movements	
		Unit 11 Structures	To enable the child to show, use and identify: 1 body tension 2 pushing and pulling against a partner to produce a balanced position 3 balance on the bar and on the floor 4 different directions and levels 5 working with a partner to produce a sequence of travelling and balancing movements	
	Unit 12 To enable the child to develop mimetic movement into dance	L.S. Lowry's paintings	To enable the child to show, use and identify partner work using: 1 accuracy of timing 2 meeting and parting 3 canon and synchronisation 4 contrasting spatial relationships with a partner 5 contrasting levels and directions	

The end of Key Stage descriptions can clearly be addressed by the above objectives.

'Pupils find solutions, sometimes responding imaginatively, to the various challenges that they encounter in the different areas of activity. They practise, improve and refine performance, and repeat series of movements they have performed previously, with increasing control and accuracy. They work safely alone, in pairs and in groups, and as members of a team. They make simple judgements about their own and others' performance, and use this information effectively to improve the accuracy, quality and variety of their own performance. They sustain energetic activity over appropriate periods of time, and demonstrate that they understand what is happening to their bodies during exercise.' – Draft National Curriculum Orders for England, 1995

Differentiation

Will this be achieved by the setting of tasks with different degrees of difficulty or will it be achieved by outcome, with everyone attempting the same task?

Progression

The elements of difficulty and quality lead directly to progression both within and between each key stage. Whereas at Key Stage 1 a child may be able to perform or compose single actions, e.g. travel, turn or jump, by Key Stage 2, the same pupil may be asked to produce these actions in combination, i.e. a travelling turning jump, thereby increasing the degree of difficulty. Progression in quality may be achieved when the teacher expects the child to perform actions with, for example, more poise, co-ordination or expressiveness than had been achieved in a former performance.

Teaching Styles

These should be appropriate for the age and experience of the children and also the nature of the tasks set. They may consist of:
- directed teaching;
- guided discovery;
- giving the class time to practice;
- question and answer;
- reciprocal teaching, with learners working in pairs, one taking the role of learner and the other as teacher giving feedback;
- problem solving;
- pupil self-check – teacher gives criteria and pupils check their own performance against them.

Assessment

The introduction of the Order for Physical Education has made assessment a statutory requirement for each child at the end of each Key Stage. Apart from this legal requirement, there is and always has been an understandable and legitimate obligation for teachers to assess and evaluate their work with children.

As Best writes 'To fail to assess is to fail to teach properly' (D. Best, *Feeling and Reason in the Arts*, Allen and Unwin, 1985). There is clearly a public demand for assessment. Parents and employers have a vested interest in education and a right and a need to be kept informed of children's progress and attainment in all areas of the curriculum.

Teachers, too, need to assess so that they can assist the progress of children in their care and encourage them to reach their full potential. Through assessment the teacher can test the effectiveness of teaching strategies, since in some degree every assessment of a pupil is also an assessment of teacher and school. Assessment of pupils can never be statements of absolute ability, but only statements of attainment within the framework of educational opportunities that have actually been provided, with assessment reflecting the objectives of each unit of work.

Most importantly, however, pupils have a right to assessment. All need to know whether they are performing to the satisfaction of others whose judgement they value. Pupils need to know whether or not they are making progress and in which areas and how they can improve if neccessary. As stated in the *National Curriculum: Task Group on Assessment and Testing Report* (DES/Welsh Office,1988), assessment 'should be an integral part of the educational process, continually providing both "feedback" and "feedforward"'.

Assessment is taking place all the time and should not disrupt the normal teaching pattern. In gymnastics and dance it will probably be most effective when it takes place in the context of the performance of a gymnastics sequence, dance or dance phrase, rather than trying to isolate and assess separate contributory skills. It should only be necessary to break down the component parts of the performance if the child is experiencing some difficulties in its execution. This analysis can then be used to diagnose the source of the problem and help the teacher to rectify it.

Neither is it necessary to set complicated tasks to assess separately the three strands of gymnastics – planning, performing and evaluating or composing, performing and appreciating in dance. One task for gymnastics and another for dance may suffice. A dance phrase or gymnastics sequence may be made, performed and evaluated by the same pupil or one pupil may be responsible for making the phrase for others to perform and the composer and/or the performer(s) to evaluate.

Neither is it necessary always to assess each of the three strands in both gymnastics and dance. The following example demonstrates this point, with performance being assessed in dance, while appreciation is assessed in gymnastics, and composition may be assessed in either gymnastics or dance.

Teaching/learning objectives

The teaching/learning objectives for this particular unit of work were to enable the child to show use and identify:
1 body tension, i.e. light/strong/relaxed movement qualities;
2 some of the compositional possibilities of working with a partner.

Some assessment possibilities

1 Performance (dance): can the child show strong movements?
2 Appreciation/evaluation (gymnastics): can children describe different relationships they have used when working with a partner, e.g. leading and following?
3 Composition/planning (dance or gymnastics): with

teacher guidance, have children made a dance/gymnastics sequence which shows some compositional possibilities of working with a partner, e.g. canon and unison?

Recording attainment

The key to effective teaching in gymnastics and dance relies on keen observation by the teacher. This is also the key to effective assessment. Both activities are ephemeral in nature and unless they are captured on video, teachers have to observe and mentally store much information about their pupils' achievements to be recalled and recorded when possible. Evidence to support assessment of performance, composition and appreciation/evaluation must all be kept. This will probably be in the form of written records made by the teacher, but may include other material provided by the pupils themselves.

The end of Key Stage 1 descriptions asks the child to 'talk about what they and others have done'. Evidence to support this statement may be gathered orally through spontaneous or planned discussion; through question and answer; or from descriptions of either the pupil's own work or that of a peer. Descriptions may also be written or recorded describing what the children have seen as fully as possible or they may focus on a particular aspect of the work, e.g. the action, spatial, dynamic or relationship features.

Similarly, evidence may also be gathered from drawings or diagrams produced by the pupils. Diagrams are particularly useful in plotting the pathways or floor patterns of dance phrases or gymnastics sequences (see page 16).

The same methods of evidence collection may be used to support the statement concerned with evaluation at the end of Key Stage 2, which deals with pupils evaluating their own and other people's performances and suggesting ways to improve that performance. Evidence can also be collected through reciprocal teaching, with pupils working in pairs swapping the roles of teacher and learner. Feedback can then be written, collected orally or from teacher observation.

Assessment in dance and gymnastics is not always an easy task to undertake, but it is necessary and should be a right for everyone concerned. It must be achieved with as much objectivity as possible and with a great degree of sensitivity, knowledge and understanding on the part of the assessor.

It may be helpful when devising any assessment plan to take the following points into account:
- The important must be assessed rather than making the assessable important.
- Assessment should take place without disrupting the normal dance and gymnastics programme.
- Assessment should be formative as well as summative.
- Assessment tasks should be devised by teachers to meet the needs of the pupils they teach, with the programmes of study and end of Key Stage descriptions acting as guidelines.

Above all, assessment should provide encouragement and motivation to reach the highest level of attainment for both pupils and teachers alike. A suggested assessment and recording system can be found on pages 17–27.

Assessment evidence: examples of children's own work

A pupil's description of her own composition.

Feets too Big

1 Starting position on floor without feet touching the floor.

3 x 8 + 8 counts to stand.

On my tummy wave legs in the air. (First Eight.)

On my back wave body and legs in the air. (Second Eight.)

On my arms wave legs in the air. (Third Eight.)

Rock forward get up and spin, then jump into a star shape.

2 3 tentative steps (weight back). Big step on 4th count transferring weight forward. Repeat on other foot then x 4 in 2 counts.

3 Chorus

Step, close, step R,L,R with loose legs and shoulders circling. Toes in then out x 4 travelling sideways.

Repeat to other side.

4 My own sequence 2 x 8

I wobble and put my knees in then I teeter, fall over and roll sideways. Then get up and lift my leg and put it down.

5 Chorus.

6 Same as before but travel in different directions.

I was thinking that I was wearing big trainers and small high-heels.

My movements are wobbling, rolling, falling, shaking and teetering.

In my dance I zigzag and travel sideways.

I move fast and slow and strong.

Louise, aged 10 years.

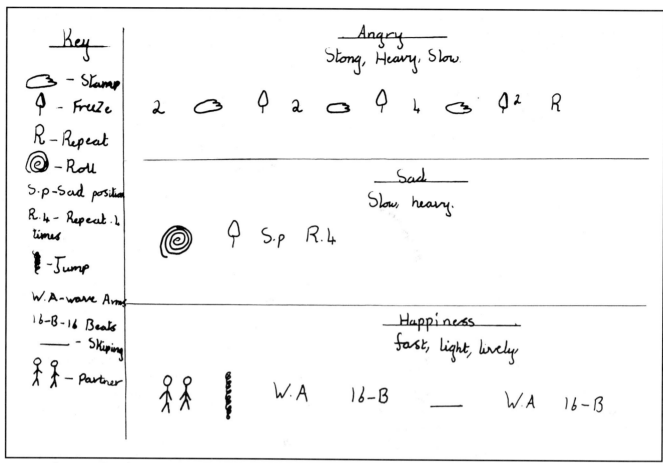

Dance diagram by Christopher, aged 9 years.

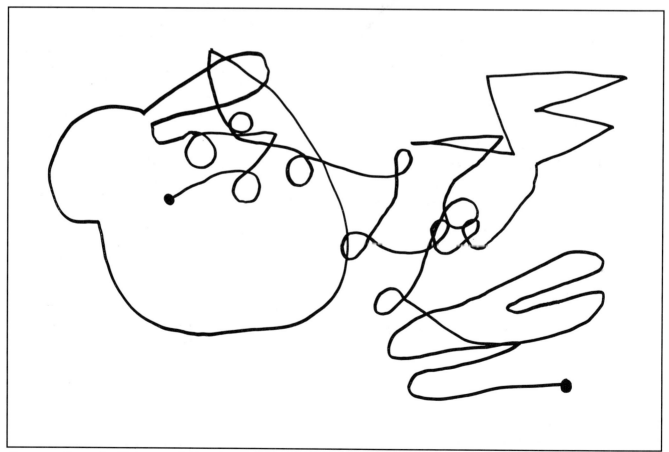

Dance pathway by Claire, aged 10 years.

A pupil's evaluation of her partner's dance.

Feets Too Big

Evaluating my Partner's Dance

1 Did my partner use different levels?

My partner used different levels like at the beginning she used low levels. Later on in the dance she used medium and high levels.

2 Did they use contrasts of speed?

At the beginning she was very slow but when she got on to her 4 lots of 8 she speeded up. Then near the end of the dance she used a steady pace.

3 Did they travel in different directions?

Her directions were very good except she went round in a squashed circle. She used forwards and backwards and diagonally.

4 During their 'shoe' section, could I tell what their original ideas were? Were they fulfilling the task set?

My partner I felt was fulfilling the task set. I could tell that she was doing a dance about feet. I could also tell that she was in high heels and large shoes. I thought that my partner had good arm swinging but was a bit lazy on the 1, 2, 3 and step movement. I liked the bit about my partner when she got up off the floor after she had done her 3 lots of 8 at the beginning. I thought she had an imaginative face and had good neat rolls.

Jane, aged 10 years.

Review

The schemes of work will always need to be monitored, evaluated, modified and developed if and when appropriate, according to the changing circumstances and experiences of the teachers and children concerned.

A description of the mechanism for the reviewing process should therefore be included in the policy document.

Assessment and recording: a suggested system*

Planning is at the centre of the assessment, recording and reporting process and the following system has been designed around that premise.

This system has been developed, tested and modified specifically for teachers of PE. It is now being used extensively and is providing much positive feedback. Some teachers have used it exactly as written while others have adapted it to meet the needs of their school. The system comprises a unit front page, which shows the contents and intention of the unit of work and an assessment record sheet, which is a simple continuous assessment document. A blank unit front page and a completed unit front page can be found on pages 20 and 21–3. An Assessment Record Sheet appears on pages 24–5, with a partially completed example on pages 27–8.

The unit front page has been designed to :
- aid the teacher in the planning of the unit structure;
- identify the relevant programmes of study;
- record the appropriate end of Key Stage descriptions directly relating to the unit.

When the unit front page is completed it can be retained as a permanent record of the work experienced by the class. It can also be used at the end of each Key Stage to check that all programmes of study and end of Key Stage requirements have been covered.

This document provides teachers with tangible evidence of their coverage of the National Curriculum and can be produced at any time.

To minimise the amount of writing required, teachers need to make their National Curriculum Orders into a master or key for identifying the programmes of study and end of Key Stage descriptions.

The end of Key Stage descriptions may be identified by the letters A, B, C, etc. The corresponding programmes of study can be identified with the letters, e.g. a, b, etc.

The Assessment Record Sheet is designed to fit an A3 paper, folded in half for easy filing. The information at the top of the Assessment Record Sheet corresponds closely to that on the unit front page.

* *Source:* Val Sabin, *A Practical Guide to Planning, Assessment, Recording, Recording and Reporting in Physical Education* (Val Sabin Publications, 1994).

The names of the class are entered in the appropriate boxes. At the completion of each lesson in the unit of work teachers may make any necessary comments beside the names of children they have assessed. Gradually, throughout the unit of work all the children will be assessed and the results recorded. However, towards the end of the unit teachers may find it necessary to take the sheet into the lesson to complete any outstanding assessments. (Those who find meeting the criteria most difficult will usually be assessed last in order to give them maximum time to achieve.)

It is not necessary or indeed desirable to record the assessment of every unit of work for each class. It is, however, advisable to update and record any improvement the children make in subsequent units of work within the same area of activity.

Teachers have found that this system has an important advantage: it gives them the opportunity to put a personal comment by the child's name, instead of just a tick or a cross. We long ago identified the importance of recognising effort in PE and dance, as well as the child's level of attainment, and this system allows this while still fulfilling National Curriculum requirements.

The Assessment Record Sheet

The Assessment Record Sheet has been designed with the following in mind:
- Assessment should be a continuous process and integral to teaching.
- It should not be onerous, neither is it necessary to record all assessments made.
- Isolated assessment at the end of a Key Stage should be avoided.
- What to assess is left to individual teachers who can determine their own criteria related specifically to end of Key Stage descriptions.

In order for teachers to focus assessment on the end of Key Stage descriptions it is necessary to 'unpack' the descriptions as shown below.

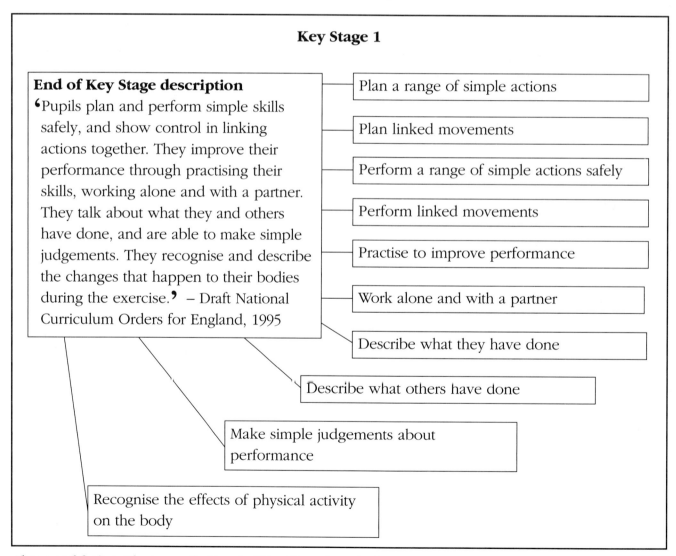

Above and facing: The 'unpacked' end of Key Stage descriptions.

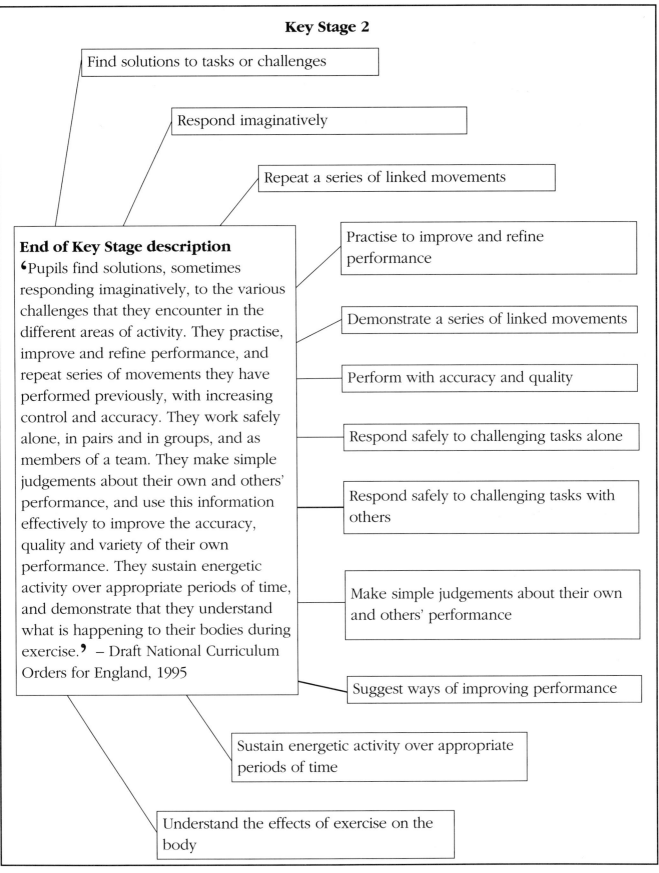

Key Stage 2

Find solutions to tasks or challenges

Respond imaginatively

Repeat a series of linked movements

End of Key Stage description
'Pupils find solutions, sometimes responding imaginatively, to the various challenges that they encounter in the different areas of activity. They practise, improve and refine performance, and repeat series of movements they have performed previously, with increasing control and accuracy. They work safely alone, in pairs and in groups, and as members of a team. They make simple judgements about their own and others' performance, and use this information effectively to improve the accuracy, quality and variety of their own performance. They sustain energetic activity over appropriate periods of time, and demonstrate that they understand what is happening to their bodies during exercise.' – Draft National Curriculum Orders for England, 1995

Practise to improve and refine performance

Demonstrate a series of linked movements

Perform with accuracy and quality

Respond safely to challenging tasks alone

Respond safely to challenging tasks with others

Make simple judgements about their own and others' performance

Suggest ways of improving performance

Sustain energetic activity over appropriate periods of time

Understand the effects of exercise on the body

Note: Children should know at the beginning of a unit of work what the points for assessment are going to be. Explain these in simple language so that all children know what they are aiming for.
Source: Adapted from Val Sabin, *A Practical Guide to Planning, Assessment, Recording and Reporting in Physical Education* (Val Sabin Publications, 1994).

UNIT FRONT PAGE

Area of activity			Unit
Class	No. in class	Age	
No. of lessons	Duration	Date to	Key Stage

Programme of study activity specific

↓

Aims

↓

Objectives

↓

Unit framework

↓

Resources

↓

Points for assessment

Source: Adapted from Val Sabin, *School Gymnastics: Key Stages 3 and 4* (Val Sabin Publications, 1993)

A completed unit front page

1 The order for filling in the front page is quite logical, and the process for completing it, simple. However, before anything else is done, the identification grid at the top of the page must be completed to allow for accurate filing.

Area of activity	Dance and gymnastics	Unit 9

Class 5J	No. in class 29	Age 9+	
No. of lessons 6	Duration 35mins	Date to	Key Stage 2

2 You may decide to have common aims and objectives for both dance and gymnastics.

> ### Aims
> 1 To explore some of the compositional possibilities of working in small groups
> 2 To increase awareness of curving and linear floor pathways
> 3 To develop the concept of enriching movement through variation

3 The aims may then be expanded into learning objectives

Objectives	Lesson 1		Lesson 2		Lesson 3		Lesson 4		Lesson 5		Lesson 6	
	Dance	Gym	Dance	Gym	Dance	Gym	Dance	Gym	Dance	Gym	Dance	Gym
To enable the child to show different ways of:												
(i) working in small groups to include:												
• meeting, parting and avoiding			[✓]		✓				✓	✓	✓	✓
• canon and unison	[✓]		[✓]		✓		✓		✓	✓	✓	✓
• copying							✓		✓	✓	✓	✓
• making group shapes and formations							✓	✓			✓	✓
(ii) enriching movement by varying speed, size and level.	[✓]		✓	✓	✓	✓		✓		✓		
To improve the child's ability to show, use and identify the use of:												
• linear and curving pathways	[✓]		✓		✓	✓	✓			✓	✓	✓
• curved and straight body shapes		[✓]	✓		✓	✓		✓				
• twisting						✓		✓	✓	✓		
• turning				✓		✓		✓		✓		
• balancing		[✓]	✓		✓		✓		✓			✓
• jumping		✓	✓				✓		✓			

Key: [✓] a main emphasis in the lesson   ✓ an emphasis in the lesson

4 The unit content should be completed next. This comprises the material and skills that may be used to achieve the objectives. It could also include possible teaching strategies. Some schools have identified specific programmes of study which are being addressed each week. However you choose to complete this section, it must be written to suit your needs.

Dance framework

I Space Invaders

1 Individual sequence of sideways travel, explode, fall, roll and stand.
2 Ways of meeting, parting and avoiding, using linear and curving pathways.
3 Canon and unison, using ideas from sections 1 and 2.

II Spaghetti

1 Using linear pathways:
   (i)   meet your partner
   (ii) use follow my leader to travel and copy each other's still shapes
   (iii) make an extended linear shape in contact with each other.
2 Travel to finish in a group of four to make a linear group structure.
3 Using twisting and turning and curving, spiralling pathways, travel showing some of the various combinations possible when working in a group of four.
4 Finish in a 'fearful tizz' whether alone, in pairs, a trio or in a group of four.

Gymnastics framework

1 Balancing to demonstrate straight lines close to/far away from floor. Jumps, spins and rolls to show straight pathways on floor/in air. Individual sequence.
2 Individual sequence-linking movements. Begin to look at curled shapes, balancing turns and spins.
3 Explore twisted body shapes, front/back/side towards the floor. Join together three different balances.
4 Twisted shapes in the air. Join together twisted jump, rolls/spins and balance.
5 Working with a partner to make combined twisted balances. Short sequence in twos to use combined twisted balances and travelling in different directions.
6 Working in groups of three, make a twisted group balance showing three different levels. Find ways of getting into and out of the balance.

---

5 Resources will follow naturally once the material has been identified.

Resources

I   Space Invaders. Music.
II   Spaghetti. 'Spaghetti' by Noel Petty; cooked and dry spaghetti, and music if required.

Resources

Mats, benches, small movable apparatus. Large apparatus. Diagrams of different linear and curving patterns and shapes.

Points for assessment

Can the child:
1 plan/compose a sequence/dance with a partner or small group to show curving and linear pathways?
2 demonstrate a sequence of movements/dance with a partner or group showing accuracy of pathway?
3 describe the sequence/dance of another pair or group and make at least one suggestion as to how it could be improved?

---

6 Remember that sometimes assessment possibilities may overlap between the activities, as in the example shown above, and sometimes you may choose to assess each activity separately.

The appropriate letters used to identify the programmes of study, activity specific, in the National Curriculum Order are entered next. This will now follow easily since the content of the unit has been identified in detail.

Programmes of study (dance)

a / b / c

Programmes of study (gymnastics)

a / b / c

The programmes of study for dance and gymnastics are detailed below.

2 Gymnastic activities

Key Stage 1

a different ways of performing the basic actions of travelling using hands and feet, turning, rolling, jumping, balancing, swinging and climbing, both on the floor and using apparatus;

b to link a series of actions both on the floor and using apparatus, and how to repeat them.

Key Stage 2

a different means of turning, rolling, swinging, jumping, climbing, balancing and travelling on hands and feet, and how to adapt, practise and refine these actions, both on the floor and using apparatus;

b to emphasise changes of shape, speed and direction through gymnastic actions;

c to practise, refine and repeat a longer series of actions, making increasingly complex movement sequences, both on the floor and using apparatus.

3 Dance

Key Stage 1

a to develop control, co-ordination, balance, poise and elevation in the basic actions of travelling, jumping, turning, gesture and stillness;

b to perform movements or patterns, including some from existing dance traditions;

c to explore moods and feelings and to develop their response to music through dances, by using rhythmic responses and contrasts of speed, shape, direction and level.

Key Stage 2

a to compose and control their movements by varying shape, size, direction, level, speed, tension and continuity;

b a number of dance forms from different times and places, including some traditional dances of the British Isles;

c to express feelings, moods and ideas, to respond to music, and to create simple characters and narratives in response to a range of stimuli, through dance.

Source: Draft National Curriculum Orders for England, 1995

ASSESSMENT RECORD SHEET

Key Stage	Area of activity

Unit	Assessment possibilities: Dance (DA)
Date:	

1	2	3	4
9	10	11	12
17	18	19	20
25	26	27	28

? = working towards **✓ = can do** **✓✓ = can do well**

Class	No. in class	Age

Unit	Assessment possibilities: Gym (GY)
Date:	

5	6	7	8
13	14	15	16
21	22	23	24
29	30	31	32

Source: Adapted from *School Gymnastics : Key Stages 3 and 4* (Val Sabin Publications, 1993)

ASSESSMENT RECORD SHEET

Key Stage	Area of activity

Unit	Assessment possibilities: Dance (DA)
	1. Compose a dance with a partner or small group to show curving and linear pathways.
Date:	2. Demonstrate a dance with a partner or group showing accuracy of pathway.
	3. Describe the dance of another pair or group and make at least one suggestion as to how it could be improved.

1	2	3	4
JAMES Da = 1 ✓✓ 2 3✓✓ Gy = 1 2✓✓ 3 Very imaginative	JANE Da = 1 2 3✓✓ Gy = 1✓ 2? 3✓✓ Needs to show more clarity of floor pathway	JOHN Da = 1 2✓ 3? Gy = 1 2 3? Can describe movement but has difficulty in suggesting improvement	
9	10	11	12
17	18	19	20
25	26	27	28

? = working towards   ✓ = can do   ✓✓ = can do well

Class	No. in class	Age

Unit	Assessment possibilities: Gym (GY)
Date:	1. Plan a sequence with a partner or small group to show curving and linear pathways. 2. Demonstrate a sequence of movements with a partner or group showing accuracy of pathways. 3. Describe the sequence of another pair or group and make at least one suggestion as to how it could be improved.

5	6	7	8

13	14	15	16

21	22	23	24

29	30	31	32

Source: Adapted from Val Sabin, *School Gymnastics : Key Stages 3 and 4* (Val Sabin Publications, 1993)

3 Planning for Dance and Gymnastics

Planning for dance

When faced with the idea of planning lessons, the first questions that normally arise are: 'Where do I begin? Should I start with the movement idea or with a dance stimulus? Do I consider first of all what children need to learn, or improve upon, in movement terms: for example, jumping, or the use of space, or do I try to find an idea or stimulus related to the class topic work? Or do I just try to begin with any idea, whether or not it is related to classroom work?' Obviously, there are no correct answers to these questions. You have to do what is most appropriate in each situation.

What is vital, however, is that the stimulus or starting point motivates the children to want to dance. It must excite you as a teacher and be meaningful to the children. Whatever you decide you should bear in mind the previous dance experience of the children and their physical, intellectual and social stages of development, together with the dance programmes of study and end of Key Stage statements.

It is also important not to contrive to make dance 'fit in' with classroom activities if it is not appropriate to do so. If you are not comfortable with the dance, then the children will not be either.

Stimuli for dance

It may be useful to look at the different stimuli that can be used. A stimulus has been defined as 'something that arouses the mind or spirits or incites activity' and Jacqueline Smith, in her book *Dance Composition* (Lepus Books, 1976), has categorised the various stimuli as follows:

1 Auditory
2 Visual
3 Kinaesthetic
4 Tactile
5 Ideational.

It is possible to add olfactory and gustatory stimuli to this list, but while these might incite activity and arouse the children it might be more difficult for young children to interpret them in dance terms.

Obviously, the classification of stimuli is only loosely used, since many stimuli, e.g. poetry, natural objects and sculpture, could be found in more than one category, depending on how they are being presented as a stimulus.

1 Auditory stimuli

The most usual auditory stimulus is probably music and it is often the first thought of many people when choosing a stimulus for a dance. You may work very closely with the music, structuring your dance according to the overall musical form, or you may be inspired by other aspects of the music, such as the mood or atmosphere that it creates. Sometimes the music may be used as a springboard for the dance idea, but then it may not necessarily be used for the final accompaniment for the dance.

There are many kinds of musical stimuli and teachers should try to introduce their pupils to as many styles as they possibly can, thereby broadening children's musical as well as dance experience. Children of primary school age respond readily to music from a variety of cultures, particularly if the pieces of music are fairly short with rhythmic vitality and clarity of phrasing. Very young children enjoy using nursery rhymes and action songs, both as a stimulus and as an accompaniment for their dance.

Percussion instruments often provide an auditory stimulus, either being used rhythmically or for the quality of movement that different instruments inspire. They fit roughly into three categories, including those which are shaken, e.g. maracas or tambourines, those which are beaten or tapped, e.g. wood blocks or tambours and those which give a more melodic sound when played, e.g. chime bars and glockenspiels. Ideally, you should have one instrument from each group, so that you can create a whole range of sounds and rhythmic patterns which can be used both as a stimulus and/or as an accompaniment for dance.

The human voice, percussive body sounds, such as clapping, clicking or stamping, or sounds in nature or the environment can also be used effectively, both as stimuli and to accompany dance. The sound of a cat purring or a police siren will stimulate very different actions and movement qualities or dynamics.

In addition, poetry can be used as an accompaniment for dance and as an auditory stimulus when the rhythm of the words or the qualitative manner in which they are said excites the movement (see the lessons based on 'Cat' by Eleanor Farjeon on pages 91–4).

2 Visual stimuli

Pattern, shape, colour, line are all sources of inspiration for dance and can be found in the world about us as well as in pictures and sculptures. The twisted roots of a tree, the spiral pattern of a shell or the shape of doors and windows in the dance space itself can all spark off dance ideas. Abstract patterns, with the emphasis on colour and shape, may stimulate a dance based on dynamics and a variety of air and floor pathways.

The sculptures of Henry Moore were the starting point for a project based on holes and cavities with Year 5 children. Some of the sculptures such as 'Three Rings' and 'Bird Basket' promoted dances based on the shapes of the sculptures, together with the contrast in dynamics suggested by the different materials used in their construction. Other sculptures such as 'Reclining Connected Forms' inspired dances based on relationships between people.

Perhaps the most exciting visual stimulus of all is that of a live dance performance by professional artists with images saying far more than words can ever do. Video recordings of professional companies also provide vivid images as starting points for the dance, as do pictures from dance books, magazines and theatre programmes. The importance of using professional dance models in a child's dance education cannot be emphasised enough.

3 Kinaesthetic stimuli

Often dances are made about movement itself, leading from the exploration and manipulation of contrasting movement ideas. A dance may evolve from a movement that the composer enjoys doing, such as turning or jumping, or it may evolve from a movement phrase, such as 'explode, travel, turn and sink'. Sometimes the particular combination of actions, dynamics, spatial and relationship features evokes dramatic overtones which, if deemed appropriate, may be developed or it may remain as pure dance with its own mood, dynamic range and form.

Watching the way other creatures move can also inspire the creation of dances. Look at birds hovering, swooping and gliding or fish that dart, glide and undulate. The gracefulness and power of lions, pumas and cheetahs seen in slow motion may also stimulate children to create dances.

Inanimate objects, such as balloons, dandelion clocks, bubbles and machinery, also have specific movement qualities which encourage children to respond with their own movements, to make dances.

4 Tactile stimuli

Different materials or objects with different textures will also suggest different ways of moving. The spiky nature of the casing of a horse chestnut might suggest sharp, sudden movements to young children, while smooth, sustained, curving movements might be suggested after the horse chestnut has lost its outer coating.

Putting their hands into a bag containing cold, cooked spaghetti certainly acted as a stimulus for a class of children who responded, after their initial surprise, with smooth, slithering movements.

Some tactile stimuli, such as fabric, can become an accompanying prop, manipulated by the dancers to form an integral part of the dance.

5 Ideational stimuli

The list here is almost endless, ranging from literature, including stories, poetry and plays to recipes; from myths and legends to scientific or mathematical concepts.

Television and comic book characters, emotions, feelings, the natural world and the technological world are all rich sources of inspiration.

Developing the dance idea

Whatever the starting point, the stimulus should be full of movement possibilities. While it is possible to make a dance about almost anything, some ideas lend themselves more easily to dance than others. Does the idea suggest contrasting movement ideas with a variety of actions, dynamics, spatial features or relationships? If it does, then the next stage is to write down any movement words or ideas related to the theme. It might then be useful to ask the following questions related to the stimulus:

1 What does it look like?

2 What does it do?

3 How does it move?

4 Where does it move?

Fireworks: a starting point for lesson planning

Bearing in mind the above questions, let us look at the idea of fireworks as a starting point for lesson planning.

1 What does a firework look like?

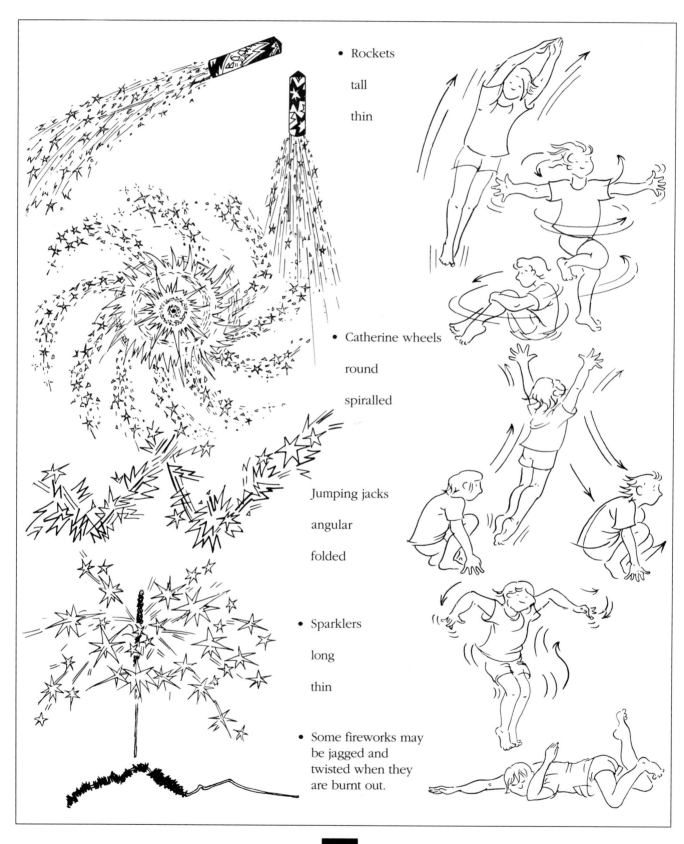

- Rockets

  tall

  thin

- Catherine wheels

  round

  spiralled

  Jumping jacks

  angular

  folded

- Sparklers

  long

  thin

- Some fireworks may be jagged and twisted when they are burnt out.

2 What do fireworks do?

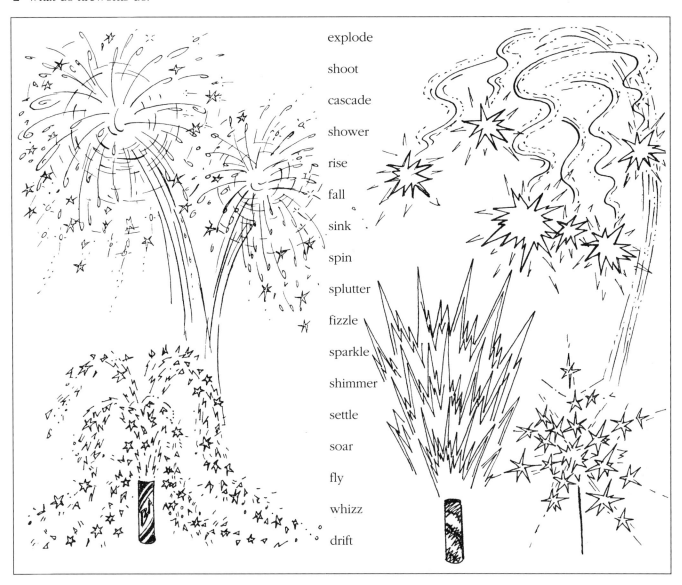

explode

shoot

cascade

shower

rise

fall

sink

spin

splutter

fizzle

sparkle

shimmer

settle

soar

fly

whizz

drift

3 How do fireworks move?

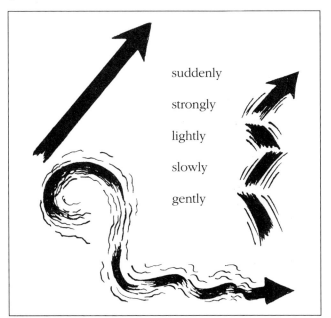

suddenly

strongly

lightly

slowly

gently

4 Where do they move?

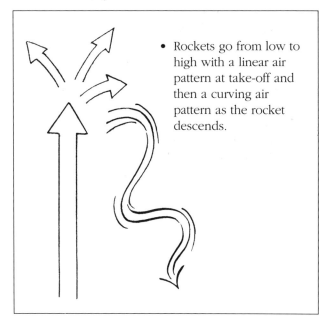

- Rockets go from low to high with a linear air pattern at take-off and then a curving air pattern as the rocket descends.

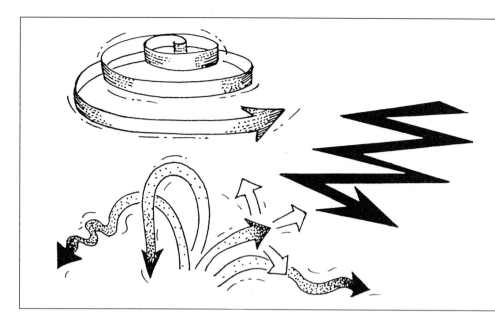

- Catherine wheels make spiralling and circular air patterns.

- Jumping jacks make zigzag patterns along the floor.

- Sparklers make a variety of air patterns.

Next decide if there are movement possibilities in the list. What actions are inherent within the words? Some are already obvious, e.g. rise and sink, soar and fly. Some, such as explode, also have dynamic connotations suggesting strong, sudden movements, while sparkle and shimmer may suggest much lighter ones. Inherent within the idea are the shapes of the fireworks – tall and thin for the rockets and sparklers and round for catherine wheels. The main spatial features suggested by the idea may be the use of different levels and a variety of air and floor patterns or pathways.

At this point, you may have too many ideas, so you will need to discard some of them or use them to make a series of lessons.

Select the most important movement ideas for your class, depending on their experience and development and visualise what you are going to ask the children to do, how they are going to do it, where and with whom. For example, an exploding rocket may suggest a sudden strong leap into the air, making a tall thin shape at the take-off and spreading into a wide shape at its height, while stars falling from the rocket may suggest soft, floating movements.

Obviously, you will not usually prescribe every movement as you will also be using suggestions from the children. You will, however, need to give clear guidelines within which the children can explore the movement ideas and make them their own.

Accompaniment

As you are visualising the movements you may decide on the sort of accompaniment that might be suitable for this exploratory stage. You will probably find it easiest to use percussion instruments and your voice during the exploration. Possibly the most useful percussion instrument is the tambourine as you can play so many

different sounds on it. You can shake or bang or scrape it. You can use a beater to create strong sounds or tap it lightly with your fingers. You can play it with a wire brush or tap the wooden rim with the handle of the beater.

Perhaps the most valuable instrument of all is your own voice. By using the voice expressively, not only can the teacher suggest *what* the children are to do but also *how* they might do it. The voice can stimulate different qualities of movement or it can be the rhythmic accompaniment to the action. Onomatopoeic words (plop, whizz, pitter patter) are particularly effective with young children, as are vocal sounds. Young children enjoy using their own voices while they dance causing their movements to come alive. This was very much the case during the movement exploration based on the idea of snow (see pages 94–5).

If you decide to accompany the class yourself, it is important to practise the accompaniment beforehand, imagining that the class is in front of you. As you become more experienced, you will possibly find that you can improvise the accompaniment during the lesson.

Structuring and accompanying the dance

Once exploration has taken place and the children have experienced some movement ideas and possibilities inherent within the theme, they should be encouraged to organise their material into a coherent pattern or form. During the exploration of the movement material the children have probably been *dancing*, but once this material is given structure and shape and the ultimate concern is with the meaning of the movement, then it is a *dance* which is being made.

Ultimately it will be the pupils who make all the decisions about how the material can be manipulated into an aesthetically pleasing dance form. Young or inexperienced children, however, will probably feel safer if they have a structure within which to express their ideas. This, of course, may be decided with the children, but at the planning stage it may be helpful if the teacher makes a loose *framework* to present to the children which may be added to, modified, kept or discarded. Dance frameworks are suggested for each dance idea in the units of work in Chapter 4.

You will also need to decide on the best way of accompanying the dance itself. If music has been used as the stimulus for the dance idea, then there should be little problem as the stimulus will probably become the accompaniment. Music, however, will obviously not be the stimulus for every dance and indeed it is essential to use a variety of different stimuli for making dances with children.

It is possible to plan a dance and then find a piece of music which is suitable as an accompaniment. It is very unlikely, however, that such a piece of music will ever be found without considerably modifying the dance idea. It is tempting to select short extracts from various pieces of music and join them together, but this should be avoided at all costs. Children should be encouraged to appreciate and value music for its own sake and not merely as an accompaniment for dance. It should be listened to as the composer intended it and not chopped up and reassembled.

Martha Graham once said that she would present all her dances in silence if it were not for the fact that audiences became too fidgety and restless. While, therefore, silence is a possibility, children, especially at the beginning of their dance careers, like many audiences, also appreciate the use of sound to accompany their dances.

What then is the answer? We were particularly fortunate when working with our classes to work with a talented musician, who composed music especially for some of the dance frameworks. This music can be found on the cassette which accompanies this book.

It is possible to dance in silence for part of the dance and 'fade in' and 'out' appropriate music. Music can also be used to create an atmospheric background accompaniment, with instruments or voices being used to emphasise or strengthen particular parts of it, as discussed in the dance lessons in the 'landscape' project in Chapter 5. There are also short pieces of music that have been written especially for dance, including those used for the BBC radio dance programmes, which may prove to be useful.

Ideally, dance and music should grow together with each stimulating and enlivening the other. This is possible particularly if you work with a teacher who is especially interested in music, with the children creating both the music and the dance around a given theme. Pupils may make their own music using percussion instruments interspersed with words and sounds. They may play it live for other children in the class to dance to, or the music may be recorded so that everyone can dance at the same time.

Music, of course, is not the only means to accompany dance. Words and sounds as already discussed in this chapter are particularly effective, as is poetry. An example of a poem being used as the basis for accompaniment can be found in the work based on 'Cat' by Eleanor Farjeon on pages 91–4.

The lesson plan

At this point, you probably thought that all the planning was complete! There is, however, one more stage and this involves placing the activities in a logical order for the smooth running of the lesson. These often fall into the following pattern:

1 Introduction

The introductory activity often serves as a transition from the classroom to the dance space. It reawakens children's awareness of the space and prepares their minds and bodies for dance. With very young children, it may be best to begin with movements fairly close to the teacher to ensure the children's involvement before they use the whole of the dance space. If possible, try to relate the activities to the rest of the lesson, rather than performing exercises merely for the sake of them. By the end of the introduction the children should be pleasantly warm, may have further developed their performance skills, movement vocabulary and be attuned to dance.

2 Movement exploration

Here children are concerned with exploring some of the movement possibilities suggested by the dance idea. This may include improvising movements within clear guidelines given by the teacher, or children may want to improvise freely after discussion about the stimulus. A variety of responses should be encouraged before some are selected and refined by the children, becoming the basis for a dance or dance phrase.

3 The dance

During this part of the lesson, movement ideas are organised and given form to make a dance phrase, or part of a dance, which may be added to in subsequent lessons to become a complete dance.

4 Conclusion

This is a time for reviewing what has happened in the lesson, either through discussion or through looking at other people's dances or dance phrases. It is a time to calm the children, particularly after a very energetic session and a time to 'warm down' their bodies, ready to return to the classroom.

The above lesson plan pattern is only a suggested outline and all sections may merge into one another. The pattern will often change with a dance phrase from a previous lesson being recalled and practised before any new material for an additional dance phrase is explored, so that the pattern of the lesson might be:

1 Introduction
2 Dance phrase A recalled and practised
3 Exploration of new or additional movement ideas leading to the making of a dance phrase B
4 Performance of dance phrases A and B
5 Conclusion.

However you organise your lesson, it is essential that there should be balance within it in terms of what you ask the children to do. Try to ensure that energetic activities are interspersed with quieter ones and that movements on the spot are followed by those that travel into the space.

Allow time for children to practise and repeat activities. Be ready with teaching points to improve their performance and compositional skills and always create opportunities for children to watch and comment upon dances, dance phrases or individual dance movements.

These threads of performing, composing and appreciating should be present in each lesson, with the teacher helping children to compose and perform their own dances through a structured framework, using a variety of stimuli as a starting point and helping them to view critically their own and other people's dances

Planning for gymnastics

As in dance, there are many starting points that may be used to initiate work in gymnastics. Again, there is no right or wrong starting point, as long as children's previous experience and their physical, intellectual and social development are taken into account when the starting point is chosen.

Having identified the theme to be used as a starting point, the material that it generates needs to be broken down into manageable pieces so that learning can take place gradually and progressively. The theme then needs to be introduced and developed coherently and logically so that children can build on basic skills, knowledge and understanding, and improve their own performance and compositional ability.

It is important here to note that the setting of a wide task allows all children to answer within the limits of their own ability, but essentially these tasks should also allow the teacher to take out a specific skill when necessary, and teach it, or part of it, to the whole class. For example, the task of travelling, taking weight from feet to hands and back to feet again, would draw out original ideas from the children but could also allow the teacher to teach skills such as 'bunny hops', forward rolls, handstands or cartwheels when appropriate.

Counterbalance and countertension

Let us look at how the theme of counterbalance and countertension may be used to plan a unit of work.
The skills that need to be learned are:

- pulling away from a partner to hold a balanced position;
- pushing against a partner to hold a balanced position.

From these basic ideas we can develop balances:

- on different levels:
- where partners make different shapes from each other;
- where partners make the same shapes as each other;
- pushing/pulling against different body parts.

It would also be possible to travel into the balance and out of the balance:

- slowly/quickly;
- using high and low levels;
- matching/mirroring each other;
- using canon/synchronisation;
- smoothly or in sudden spurts

– and all could be combined into a sequence. These ideas could then be developed using small apparatus and large apparatus in a similar way.

Once all the ideas associated with the theme are explored, it is then possible to begin the process of planning and constructing a lesson.

What is the ideal structure for a gymnastics lesson? It is generally accepted that a lesson plan should have three main sections and a short calming-down activity at the end:

1 Warm-up or opening activity
2 Floorwork or movement training
3 Apparatus work
4 Calming-down activity.

Although a lesson plan is composed of these different sections, it does not mean that each section should be cut off neatly and decisively from the next, but rather each lesson should be treated as a whole, with smooth and logical transitions between sections and no discernible joins.

1 Warm-up

The warm-up has a dual purpose, preparing both body and mind for the lesson. As all parts of the body are needed for travelling activities in the gymnasium, it is logical and necessary to warm-up all body parts in preparation for receiving weight in all situations. However, preparation of the mind should not be neglected – making children concentrate their minds on specific tasks and performing simple skills helps develop and improve fine judgement. In this section complete co-ordination of mind and body should be a prime consideration.

In the warm-up actions may begin on the spot and

then develop into travelling. Once locomotion takes place, an awareness of the general space in the gym is needed; control in speed and changes of direction will be required in order to avoid others also moving in the same area. Judgement and the ability to adapt to changing situations is important and should be stressed in the last few minutes of the warm-up.

2 Floorwork

While aspects of the main theme will probably have been introduced in the warm-up, it should now be developed in some detail if it is a new area of work. If the movement idea has been introduced in a previous lesson, it will now be recalled and further developed. There is a twofold aim in this section, for teachers must attempt to provide children with experiences that will extend their knowledge and understanding of movement and of their own body potential, as well as training bodily skills. Floorwork is simply the safest way of mastering techniques and skills and exploring movement ideas in order to become totally familiar with them before applying, developing and adapting them on apparatus. The training of the body is still the main concern in this section, but it has other implications – those of understanding movement through the acquisition of skill.

Once the class acquires this knowledge and ability, then the children will be expected to use it appropriately when working in other situations, such as with a partner or on apparatus.

3 Apparatus

Here the teacher should aim for the confident and successful application of ideas and techniques learned on the floor, and the development and adaptation of those ideas in different situations. Children should be able to handle the apparatus with confidence, use it safely and recognise that the floor is also part of the apparatus in order to help free-flowing uninhibited movement of several children on one piece of apparatus at the same time with no queues. Awareness of others, general space, personal space and judgement are all an integral part of work on the apparatus.

Apparatus should be sited and selected, not only to suit the strength and experience of children in the class, but also to suit the theme being taught. The handling of apparatus should also be looked upon as an important learning process in its own right; it should be seen as an opportunity for teaching safe lifting and lowering techniques and for teaching children to work with others.

Whatever the length of the lesson, the proportion of time allocated to floor and apparatus work has to be considered. The amount of time actually spent moving can be divided into the ratios:

two thirds to one third; half and half; one third to two thirds.

When introducing a new idea, the time spent working at floor level, may be greater than that on the apparatus – two thirds to one third – but in consecutive lessons the working time will probably be equally divided. Once the particular theme has been fully explored at floor level, the children will need a greater proportion of time to exploit the possibilities on apparatus – one third to two thirds.

While the lesson plan should ideally consist of the three sections outlined above, this does not mean that every lesson has to contain both floor and apparatus work. Occasionally, it may be wise for the teacher to spend a complete lesson on floorwork because the children are interested, and the work is developing well in different ways. Similarly, there may be the occasional lesson that is spent entirely on apparatus work, e.g. when the children have been developing a theme for several lessons and they have reached the stage where they need to work for a lengthy period of time on composing movement sequences on the apparatus. You should be prepared to follow a theme and should not be dictated to by rigid immovable rules of lesson planning. Flexibility and adaptability are the key words!

4 Calming-down activity

Any quiet activity can be used. The following offer a number of suggestions:

a **Sleeping lions:** The children lie silently in a space on the floor with their eyes closed. The teacher initiates the activity by touching several children gently on their feet. When touched, the children rise quietly and each touch one other child on the foot before tiptoeing to join the queue by the door. Gradually, the queue grows until everyone is silently waiting to return to the classroom.

b **Slow motion standing:** The children lie silently in a space on the floor. The teacher counts to ten very slowly and the children take the full ten seconds to stand up slowly and silently.

c **Tiptoe over the flowers:** Everyone in the class stands silently in a space. Without making a sound they must tiptoe over the flowers to the door and line up.

d **The pied piper:** The children lie silently in a space on the floor. As the teacher tiptoes past them, they stand up quietly and silently follow the teacher. The teacher weaves in and out of the class until all the children are following and then leads them through the door!

e **Don't break the chain:** Everyone stands in a large circle holding hands, with the teacher being part of the circle. Silently, everyone tiptoes round in the circle completing one circuit before the teacher

releases the hand of the child on his/her left. The
teacher keeps on moving in the same direction, but
leads the line towards the door – the children must
remain linked. If the environment allows, the teacher
could lead the children quietly through the door and
all the way to the classroom, all without releasing hands.

Organisation of apparatus within a lesson

Having established as essential a smooth and logical
transition beween different sections of the lesson, we
arrive at a stumbling block for many teachers – the
getting out and organisation of apparatus!

One often hears teachers bemoaning the fact that
apparatus construction is so time consuming that actual
teaching time is cut to a minimum. This should not be
so, for a well-organised teacher with properly trained
children should be able to move on to the apparatus
quickly, efficiently and safely, without significantly
interrupting the flow of the lesson.

Of prime importance to the organisation process is
the need to ensure that a new class of children in the
gymnasium should initially be given as much time as is
necessary to learn the safe and efficient handling of each
piece of apparatus as it arises within the lesson. At these
times, once the correct handling has been traught,
efficiency can be tested through short games and
competitions, so that repetition and enjoyment bring
complete understanding and familiarity. A thorough
understanding and confidence in handling the apparatus
is essential in these initial stages and if properly
conducted, will enable children (with constant
reminders) to be safe and efficient in the handling of
apparatus for the remainder of their years at school.

Apparatus can be moved and used successfully by
children from the age of 4 years. In order to make this
possible, the teacher must observe the following simple
rules:

1 Be totally organised.
2 Teach children slowly and carefully the rules of lifting
   and placing apparatus.
3 Try to match complexity of layout with age and
   competence, i.e. 4- and 5-year-olds should have very
   simple layouts of apparatus and 10- and 11-year-olds
   much more complex and interesting ones.

The most important point relating to apparatus in
primary schools is that children should take out and put
away their own apparatus every lesson. One large set
should not be erected in the morning for everyone to
use in turn, because:

- the layout will not relate to the particular theme they
  are following;

- children do not experience a progression from
  floorwork on to apparatus; and
- they do not learn how to handle the apparatus for
  themselves, consequently losing out on an exciting
  and satisfying part of the lesson.

Apparatus handling

When a reception class first begins gymnastics, it will
spend several lessons learning to respond to
instructions, how to travel on feet in various ways,
identifying different body parts, how to find space and
how to use space. When children have passed through
these preliminary experiences, they can then progress to
using apparatus.

In order to facilitate easy movement of apparatus for
young children, the following basic organisational
points should be observed, if the room allows:

- Always have the mats in different corners, or at least
  in two different piles on opposite sides of the room in
  order to minimise crush.
- Benches are always more easily accessible if they are
  spread around the outside edges of the room.
- In order to prevent crush and disorder, it is helpful to
  place any main movable apparatus around the sides
  of the hall in the appropriate position. It makes life
  very difficult if all apparatus and mats are stored at
  one end of the hall or in a storeroom.

Because reception class children are so small, and the
apparatus relatively heavy, it is imperative that children
are taught the 'buddie' system of lifting, e.g. when lifting
a bench, a group of children should all work together to
ensure safety.

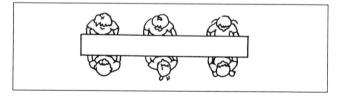

Teachers should use as many children to lift a bench as
they think necessary, but it is essential that the lifting is
conducted as follows:

1 Children are spaced along each side of the bench, not
   at the ends of the bench because this would mean a
   child having to walk backwards when carrying, and
   in the early stages this might be unsafe.
2 They all prepare (under the guidance of the teacher)
   – 'Bend knees, head up (back straight), hold the
   bench firmly.'
3 One child says clearly '1, 2, 3, lift' so all children lift at
   the same time.
4 The bench is pointed in the direction in which it is to
   travel, so no child walks backwards.

Pages 36 – 47 first appeared in Val Sabin, *Primary School Gymnastics – a Teaching Manual* (Val Sabin Publications, 1990).

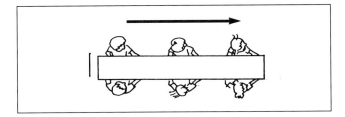

5 When the bench has been carried to its appointed place in the room, the children gently lower it to the floor and then sit down beside it.

With young children, it is advisable to move all apparatus in this way, and establish a recognised safe procedure.

Getting out apparatus

1 Children should learn to handle apparatus as soon as possible.
2 Learning to handle apparatus should be a gradual process, starting in a simple way with mats and progressing to single, simple, low pieces of apparatus.
3 When children lift a piece of apparatus they should know:
   a how many children should be holding it;
   b where they have to hold it;
   c have knees bent and a straight back ready to lift;
   d only to lift when everyone is ready.

How to carry apparatus safely

Mats

Mats require at least four carriers for lower infants – two on each side near the ends. As children become older and stronger, two carriers, one on each side, should be sufficient. **Mats should never be dragged – lift with back straight.** Travel sideways so that everyone is walking freely.

Benches

With reception and infants there could be as many as three or four children on each side and none at the ends. The bench should be pointed towards where it is to be positioned so no child walks backwards. For juniors, benches require at least two carriers – one at either end, facing each other. The ideal movement is sideways, but if travelling backwards remind children to look over their shoulder.

When carrying a heavy soft-topped bench, children should hold it under the padded rim, *not* right underneath on the wooden frame; otherwise this may lead to trapped fingers. There should also be at least two children on each side of the bench, as well as one at each end for juniors – more on the sides and none at the ends for reception children and lower infants.

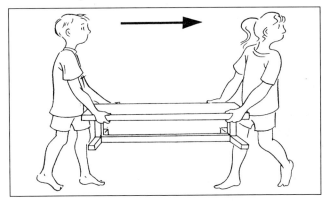

Planks, beams, ladders, parallel bars

Carriers should be positioned as for benches – hands at the sides for infants, at the ends for juniors. Check that fingers do not get trapped

Stools and small boxes

For small stools and boxes there should be two carriers – one on either side for juniors, double the numbers for reception. The movement is sideways with children facing the way they are walking. Carry on the side which is free of metal bars so toes are not damaged.

Larger boxes and movement tables

Larger boxes and movement tables require four carriers – two on either side for juniors, and the movement is sideways with children facing the way they are going.

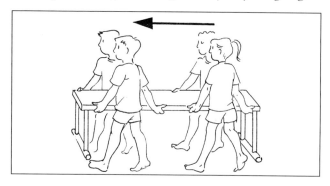

Fold-away A frames

These should be unstrapped from the wall and erected immediately. Depending upon the size of frame and size of child there may be one or two children each side of the A so toes are not trapped. Lift and carry with children walking forwards.

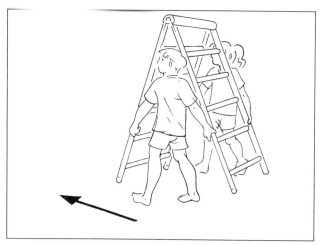

Wallbars and climbing frames

Much depends upon the design of these. Make sure children know how to get them out and secure them. Check all parts (tensioning, cables, bolts) are secure before children use them. When children move them away from the wall and into position, make sure there is a sufficient number of children involved.

Metal corner unit

Use as many children as necessary at each of the following stages:

1 Release the ladder-upright from the wall straps and place on the floor, with the floor-bolt holes about half way along it. Insert the metal 'mushrooms' into the holes.

2 Carry ladder and hook one end on to the wall-ladder. Secure with bolts.

3 Hook the other end on to the desired rung of the frame lying on the floor. Secure with bolts.

4 Once secured at both ends, lift the frame from the floor and drop on to the 'mushrooms'.

5 Secure the pole across to the corner upright.

6 Put the unit away in reverse order.

Ropes

At least four pupils are needed – two or more to guide the ropes safely and one or two to pull the ropes into position.

Remember: When apparatus is going to be taken out, remind children that:
- everyone must be quiet and listen to instructions.
- no one touches apparatus until given permission by the teacher.

Progressive introduction and use of apparatus from reception classes to top juniors

Stage 1

It is suggested that mats should be the first piece of apparatus carried and used by reception classes:

a Initially, the teacher should choose four children to pick up a mat (two on each side, not one at each corner), carry it into a space, lower it and sit at the side of it. This process should be repeated with each mat being carried by a different group of four children each time. The operation should be carried out slowly and carefully.

b Next time they get out the mats, the teacher could ask the children to hold hands with a partner, then ask two pairs to pick up a mat and carry it into a space.

c As their number recognition and perception of space improves, the teacher can ask the children to sit in front of him/her in a line of twos.

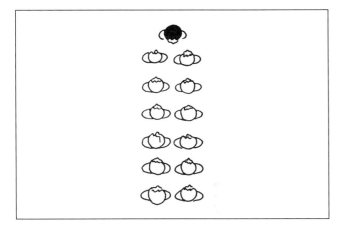

From this position the teacher can ask the first two pairs to carry a mat into a space and sit beside it, and so on down the line. Children should be able to manage this last stage of organisation quite quickly, and if the mats are in different piles, they may be taken out speedily, with no congestion.

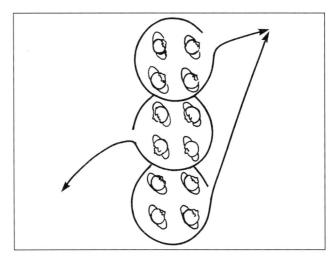

For the first two or three weeks, the apparatus section of the lesson could simply be mats set out in a space. The children could use the space around the mats, jump on to them, etc.

Stage 2

Having experienced carrying and using mats, children should next familiarise themselves with moving benches.

Some schools may have wooden benches, others may also have the padded vinyl, metal-framed benches, but whichever type of bench is moved, the same procedure should be followed as explained on page 37.

a Initially, *only* benches should be placed in the hall to allow for exploration – under, over, through, along – and for this, mats are not required because the benches are very low.

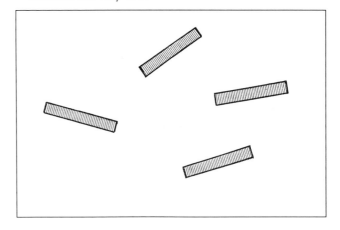

b After handling and a period of exploration, mats could be added to the benches. They should not, however, just be placed at the side or end of the bench because this leads to queueing and restricted movement.

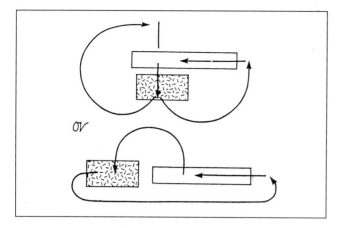

By placing the mats at an angle to the benches, children will be encouraged to show more imagination in their use of entrances and exits.

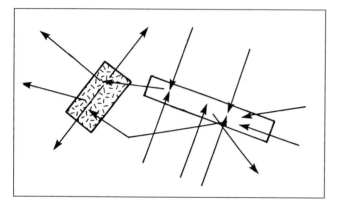

Each small group then also retains more space in which to work because it has use of bench, mat and floor area between and around them.

Even at this early stage, and at the beginning of their gymnastic experience, children should be made aware of safe placement and spacing of apparatus, and to recognise if an entrance or exit is too close to a wall or another piece of apparatus.

Although children must always get out and put away their own mat/bench, they should not be restricted to working with their own piece of apparatus. For children to learn effectively about spacing and working together, they need to be able to move around the whole area of the hall, using both floor and apparatus. With young children, who have little gymnastic experience, this whole area approach means they will also be learning (with prompting!) to work all the time and not standing in queues waiting for a turn. With this approach, the activity level of the lesson rises dramatically.

Stage 3

The third stage of apparatus handling should be the erection and use of the small A frame.

It is essential that:

a the frame be released from its wall straps and constructed immediately.

b the children should stand at the sides of the A to lift and carry it – already constructed – into position. This will ensure that toes are not damaged in the carrying. Also, if A frames are released from their wall straps and are dragged into position before erection, the stabilising rubbers will erode and the A frames will become unsafe.

With the inclusion and use of A frames and small stools/boxes, another dimension is added to the apparatus set-up – a sloping surface to travel along/over/under by hooking one end of the bench on to the A frame or supporting frame of the stool.

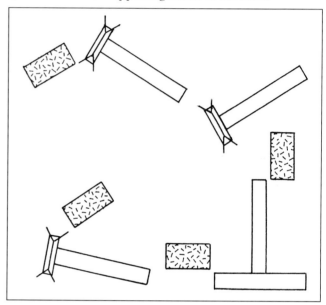

Stage 4

From these simple beginnings, it then becomes possible to add other small pieces of apparatus in different combinations to produce significantly different simple set-ups. A frames, small boxes, a fixed ladder against the wall can all combine, in different ways, to produce a surface raised above the ground, either on the level or sloping. The following offer some suggestions:

a Two A frames supporting either a padded bench, balance beam, ladder, parallel bar, red bar or pole.

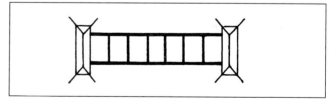

b Using the same ideas as **a** but the frames are of a different size.

c Same idea again, but the hooked-on apparatus is sloping.

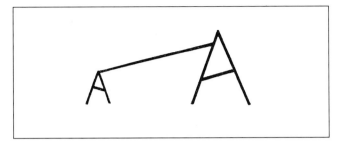

d A frame and fixed ladder can hold a raised piece of apparatus, either horizontally ...

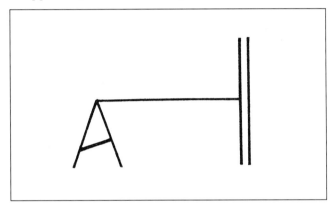

... or sloping.

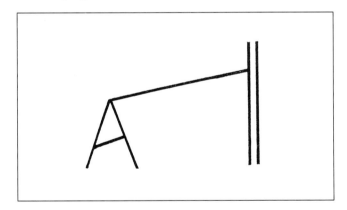

e Fixed ladder and box or stool, either horizontally ...

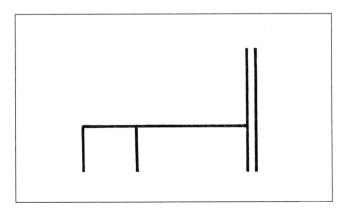

... or sloping.

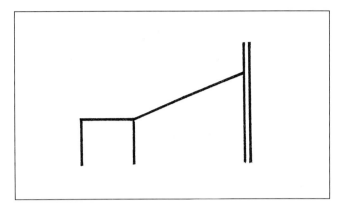

f A frame and box.

Where balance beams and poles have hooks at either end, the hooks are on a swivel, so the balance bar/poles can be placed at angles to other pieces of apparatus.

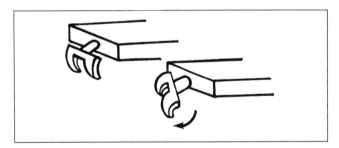

Stage 5

As classes become familiar with handling and placing apparatus, the teacher should then attempt to add angles to the layouts.

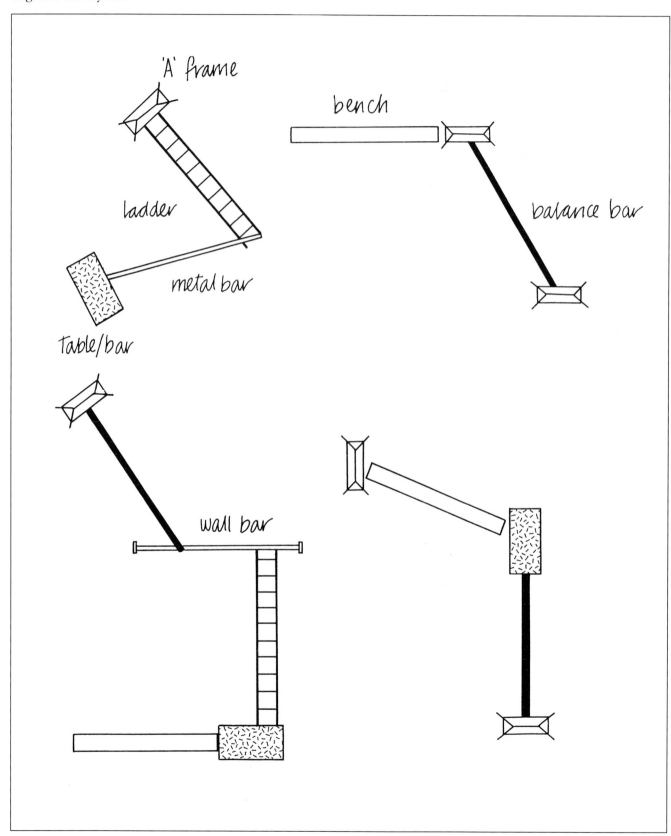

The construction of an L, T, V, Y, or N shape with apparatus will have the effect of creating more space and many more exits and entrances – quite apart from making it much more interesting to use!

Stage 6

As children develop greater competence and wider experience on apparatus, it will be helpful to remember the following point. If the working space is small and the classes large, more space will be created if the apparatus is designed to link with, or lead on to another set of apparatus. By setting a task that requires the children to move on the floor between the apparatus, as well as use the apparatus when it is free, they will be learning about spacing, relationships and co-operation with other children, as well as having a much higher activity level.

As a result of operating in this way, children may, in the early stages, tend to crowd on to a favourite piece of apparatus, so the following ideas are suggested to encourage them to spread out and become more aware of the space around them, other children and all the apparatus:

a 'Run in and out of all the apparatus without touching it.'

b 'Run in and out of the apparatus. When you come to a clear piece travel underneath it and move on.'

c 'Run in and out of the apparatus. When you come to a clear piece travel over or under it without touching it, and move on.'

d 'Travel in different ways between the apparatus (sliding, hopping, jumping, stepping, bunny-hopping, etc.) and when you come to a clear piece, travel over or under it without touching it.'

e 'Run in and out of all the apparatus. When you come to a clear piece, use it in any way once, and then move on.'

f 'Travel in and out of all the apparatus and when you come to a clear piece, balance on it for a count of "100, 200, 300" and then move on.'

Any of these ideas, plus any similar ones related to the themes being used, will prove to be most effective in helping children to adjust to moving around in the larger space of the room and having to cope with both the apparatus *and* other children.

An exciting and stimulating environment can be created through imaginative use of surfaces and obstacles. Flat surfaces, inclined bars, benches, tubular ladders and parallel bars can be used and negotiated. All these pieces of equipment carefully and imaginatively arranged to suit the space available equals a successful layout and a stimulating learning environment.

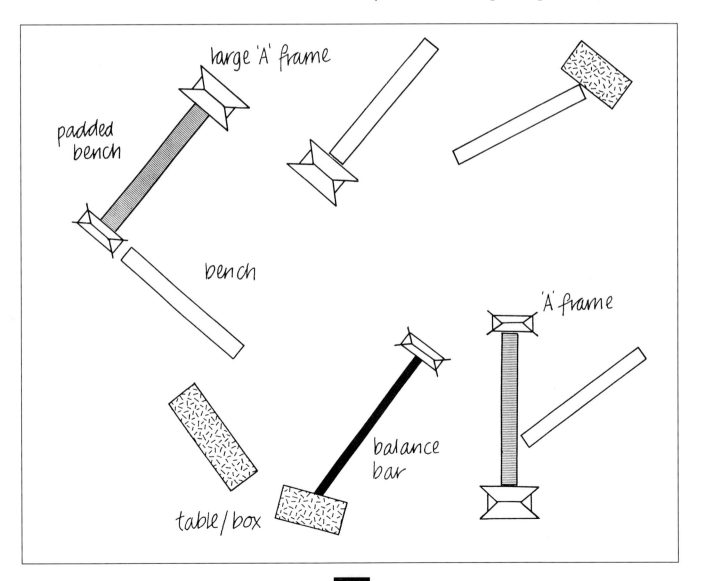

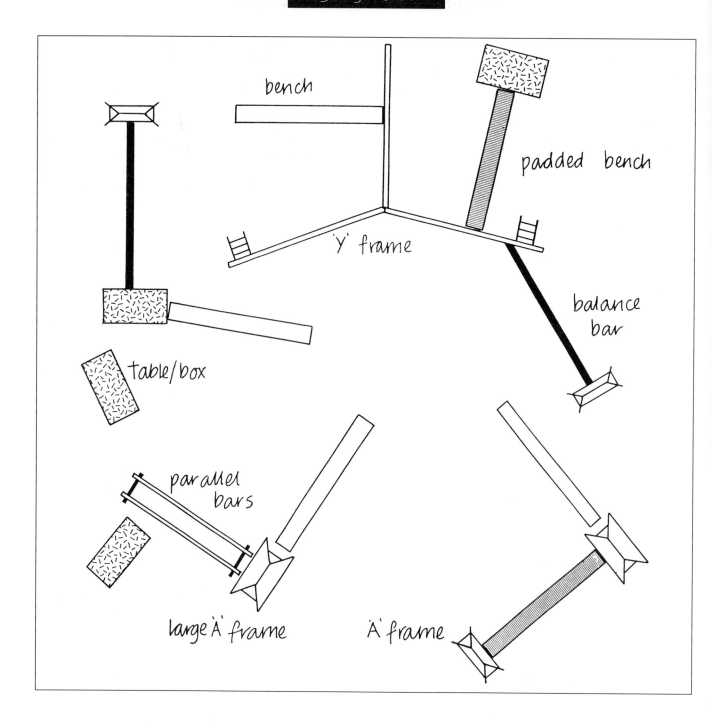

How to design an apparatus plan

Having explored the ways in which apparatus can be built up, what is the most effective approach to creating an apparatus plan?

1 List all the apparatus available in the hall, both fixed and movable.
2 Draw an empty box roughly the same proportions as the working space. Mark in the site of fixed apparatus around the walls.
3 Any fixed apparatus, e.g. climbing frame, Y frame or corner unit, must be erected in its own area, so the plan should begin with the arrangement of these pieces.

4 Tick off the items of apparatus on your list as they are included in the plan.
5 Leave the benches, planks and smaller items of apparatus until the large and fixed pieces are sited, because it will then be easier to work out where they can be hooked and which apparatus pieces will link together.
6 Try to think of fresh ideas. Don't always link together the same pieces of apparatus.
7 Always build up the plan around the optimum number of groups for the space. The linking apparatus can be added when the main groups of apparatus have been planned.

The number of possibilities available to the teacher when creating apparatus plans are innumerable. It is important to be imaginative since a well thought-out apparatus plan can last for approximately half a term or the duration of a theme.

The following idea has been helpful:

a Several members of staff stay behind one evening and experiment with how different pieces of apparatus can successfully and safely link on to one another.

b As the staff set up ideas, someone draws a plan of each set-up and another member of staff takes photographs.

c In about 40 minutes, with several people involved, many different apparatus groups can be discovered and recorded. The plans and photographs can be kept in a folder in the staff room to help stimulate ideas for class apparatus plans.

Organisation for setting up apparatus

1 Simple sets of benches and mats

a If children have been working on the floor, with no mats.
  i Sit children in groups where the apparatus is to be placed.
  ii If benches are placed around the room, tell each group from where it collects its bench and in which position it is to be placed; then ask them to sit down beside it.
  iii Tell two groups at a time to collect and place their mats in position; then set the first task.

b If children have been working on mats and they are already out:
  i Make sure the mats are placed in a good space.
  ii Instruct the children from where they collect their benches and where they position them. Tell them to place the bench and sit down. Set the first task.

2 More complex apparatus plans

a If children have been working on the floor and there are no mats out.
  i Sit children in groups where the apparatus is to be placed.
  ii Tell each group which large piece of apparatus it will be using and where it is to be placed. Everyone takes out their large piece of apparatus and then sits down.
  iii Tell each group which smaller pieces it will be adding to the apparatus and where they will be placed. Remind them that mats must be added last. Everyone gets out their remaining apparatus, checks it and sits down.

b If mats are already out.
  i If there are to be four groups, divide the mats into four groups and place them quickly in a pile in the four areas. (Children are directed to take their mat to a corner and stay there with their group.)
  ii Take out the large piece of apparatus as above.
  iii Add the small pieces and rearrange the mats with the apparatus.

c When children have experienced taking out a set-up of apparatus slowly and in sections, as above, next time they may only need reminding which apparatus they take out, and in which order, before being given instructions to proceed.

The main points again . . . setting up apparatus

1 It is most important when children are learning how to handle a new piece of apparatus that they should be allowed as much time as necessary to learn it safely and efficiently.

2 The first time a class of children takes out a more complex set of apparatus, it must be taken out slowly – stage by stage:
  a Large piece of apparatus first;
  b Benches and small pieces next;
  c Mats into place last.

3 As children become more familiar with the set-up, they need not be directed at each stage, merely questioned and reminded:
  a which apparatus is being taken out;
  b in which order it is taken out.
  Then they may be allowed to take out the apparatus, with the teacher moving between the groups and watching carefully, helping where necessary. The children should sit down when the apparatus is out and they have checked it.

Putting away apparatus

1 Children should always put away the set of apparatus that they took out. They should return the pieces to the same part of the room from where they collected them.

2 When putting apparatus away, the order of moving it should be reversed, i.e. children should always put away:
  a mats first;
  b benches and small apparatus next;
  c large apparatus last.
  This allows the floor to be cleared in order to move the awkward or heavy pieces of apparatus more easily and without obstruction.

3 As apparatus is put away, it should be returned to its original storage position *neatly*.

Formation and use of groups within the apparatus section

1 Children should be divided into apparatus groups according to the size of the room. Within each group, there could be a leader, but ultimately the teacher must check everything before it is used.

2 Groups should remain the same each week for the duration of a theme. Established groups help strengthen discipline and control. Each group will become able to handle and site their own apparatus quickly and efficiently.

3 Children should always sit quietly in their groups and await instructions.

4 Groupings for apparatus could be allocated in some of the following ways:

   a If there are to be five groups, children can sit in a space on the floor and the teacher gives everyone a number (1 – 5); then No. 1s are asked to stand up and go to a particular area of the room, etc.

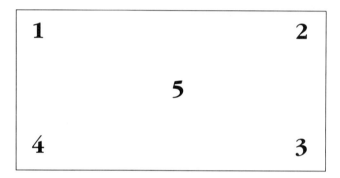

   b If there are 30 children in the class, the children could sit down in a space, the teacher counts six children and sends them to one part of the room, another six to a second part, etc.

   c Children are asked to sit in pairs in a line in front of the teacher: the first three pairs are directed to one corner, etc.

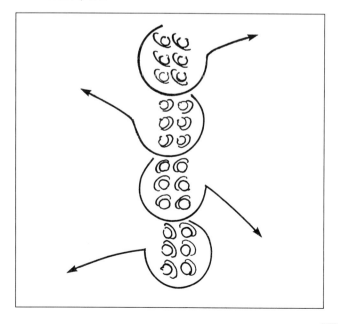

   d The teacher could identify each group with a colour and then send each one to a different corner.

   e Groups of children on different tables in the classroom make up the apparatus groups.

   f If children have mats out, the teacher could ask them to carry their mat to a corner and stay there, etc.

However groups are allocated, it is important that the selection should only occur at the beginning of a half-term or theme. It is good to change the method of selection so that children do not always work with the same people.

Once they have been allocated groups, children will be expected to work co-operatively within them and take out their own sets of apparatus safely and efficiently.

Rotation

Once the apparatus has been taken out, many teachers still favour the rotation of groups on apparatus. Each group:

a takes out its own set of apparatus;
b warms up on its own apparatus;
c rotates round to the next set of apparatus and works on that;
d goes back to its own apparatus and puts it away.

Does this approach give children a basic security or could it be considered too restrictive? Could it cause queuing and taking turns? Does it demotivate children by giving them a sense of unfairness that they have not been able to use a particular piece or apparatus?

Whole area

The whole area approach is favoured by many teachers, for younger, less experienced children and older, more mature and talented children, whereby groups:

a take out their own set of apparatus;
b warm up and explore all the apparatus and floor area;
c work on tasks that encourage the use of all the floor and apparatus;
d return to their own set of apparatus and put it away.

The environment here is stimulating; children feel they have really used all the apparatus; it encourages the development of spatial awareness and co-operation among children; it prevents queuing; and while there is an unrestricted feeling, the requirement to fulfil a task encourages a situation of controlled freedom.

Rotation/whole area

In this combination children:

a work in groups to take out their own set of apparatus;
b warm up using all the floor and apparatus;

c work in their group and rotate to the next one;

d return to their group to put away the apparatus.

They have the stimulation of being able to use all the apparatus to warm up and for simple tasks; unrestricted free use of space – no queuing; the opportunity to discover many exits and entrances to the apparatus, with the security of returning to the stability of their own group and a set of apparatus in order to produce sequences or sets of movements.

Could this be an effective way of working with top juniors?

Obviously, individual teachers will decide which approach they wish to take with a class, but by breaking down the approaches in this way, it can be seen that different ones might be appropriate at different stages in a child's development. Similarly, the approach might alter from one week to another, e.g. high winds might make a class really restless and overstrung, so perhaps the highly structured rotation approach might be the most appropriate for that particular day.

We should be aware of the different approaches available in the apparatus section of the gymnastics lesson, and then be adaptable and flexible enough to use different ones as appropriate.

Gymnastic apparatus

In order for children to participate in significant gymnastic activity, it is essential for them to experience moving, constructing and using a variety of gymnastic apparatus during their lessons. Type of environment, size of school hall, number of pupils on roll and not least, available finance, are all major factors governing the amount and variety of gymnastic apparatus available in individual schools.

This short section on types of apparatus and its uses has been included to offer guidance to schools on any future purchase of gymnastic equipment. The apparatus has been sectioned into types for ease of identification.

Mats

The most essential apparatus – basic floor skills can be safely taught on them, and the majority of apparatus could not be used safely without them – mats can be landing areas and pieces of equipment which link together various groups of apparatus.

The storage of mats can cause a problem. Ideally, mats should be stored in two different corners of the hall, giving easy access. Many schools store their mats on a trolley, and for ease and safety it should be wheeled into the centre of the hall, the mats removed, and then wheeled away.

Siting mats is a surprisingly difficult task. If a mat is placed by or underneath a piece of apparatus it is an invitation to children to jump on it. Therefore, each school needs to develop its own policy on placing mats against or underneath high apparatus. If a high piece of apparatus has been erected for the express purpose of hanging from hands, so the drop on to the floor is not great, then mats can be placed underneath it, but children must be told not to hang by knees, etc. as the landing area would be totally inadequate if they fell from that position.

If ropes are to be used for swinging upon, then mats should not be placed underneath them as children could easily trip when running between swings. However, if ropes are to be used for balancing, climbing and turning upside-down, mats are necessary.

Obviously, these are very simple guidelines, and ultimately the responsibility for mat placement lies with the individual teacher and what he/she feels is necessary for the safety of the children. An ideal number of mats could be calculated as anything beween one mat to four children and one mat to two children.

Benches

- Wooden long benches (with hooks on one end)
- Wooden short benches (with hooks on one end)
- Light alloy benches with padded tops (with hooks on one end)
- Planks – wooden or alloy – with a hook on end

Benches are extremely useful items of apparatus and invaluable aids to creating interesting sets of apparatus, particularly if they have a set of flexible hooks at one end. Benches are dual-purpose small pieces, which can be used either as free-standing apparatus or hooked on to other fixed or free-standing pieces.

Free-standing apparatus

- A frames
- Bar box
- Nest of tables
- Movement table

Included in every school apparatus store there should be some of these items of free-standing pieces, as they form the central part of any creative sets of apparatus.

Hook-on apparatus

- Balance bar
- Ladder
- Metal bars
- Parallel bars
- Large padded benches
- Benches
- Planks

With a good basic collection of free-standing pieces, these hook-on items will prove invaluable in the creation of interesting sets of apparatus. A selection of these hook-on pieces should be an essential part of the school store.

Fixed apparatus

- Wall bars
- Wall frames
- T or Y frames
- Box frame
- Ropes
- Metal corner unit

Fixed pieces of apparatus have usually been built into the structure of the hall. However, occasionally school halls lack any large fixed apparatus. Ideally, schools should have at least one of the above items, for children at primary school age need to climb and hang, and they should be given a chance to experience it in the relative safety of the school.

Children safely handling apparatus

4 Units of Work for Dance and Gymnastics

Obviously, there are many links between dance and gymnastics – after all, the body can only perform a certain number of actions – but it is the motive behind these actions and the way the movements are put together which will determine whether what results is dance or gymnastics. It does, however, make sense to stress these links, as well as differentiating between the two activities, so that sometimes similar material may appear in both gymnastics and dance lessons. We have, therefore, written units of work for both activities with similar teaching/learning objectives.

In the dance units there are usually several teaching/learning objectives during the six-week unit of work as it is very difficult to make dances or dance phrases without drawing on several aspects of movement material. The gymnastics units of work have been designed to focus more on one particular teaching/learning objective which is included in the dance objectives.

All three aspects of each activity – composing, performing and appreciating in dance and planning, performing and evaluating in gymnastics – should be apparent in every lesson, but sometimes the objectives will have a strong emphasis on only one aspect.

Sometimes you may wish to run both the gymnastics and dance units of work parallel with each other, especially with children in reception and year 1 classes. At other times you may decide to teach the gymnastics units before the dance ones, or vice versa, so that the children do not become satiated with what may appear to be similar ideas.

The units of work in both areas are only offered as suggestions and should be adapted to meet the needs of individual classes.

Cross-curricular links

While dance and gymnastics are important in their own right in a child's education, they can also provide opportunities to enhance other curriculum areas.

In primary schools, in particular, there are so many opportunities for the development of cross-curricular links and as it is usually the class teacher who is responsible for most areas of the curriculum, it is relatively easy for these links to be made, not only in the aims and content of the areas of work, but also in the way that children learn and apply their knowledge, skills and understanding. Some links are perhaps more obvious than others, including the natural affinity between dance and the other arts: for example, music and dance both seek to develop the child's natural capacity for rhythm and phrasing; dance and visual art share the same spatial relationships, while both dance and drama provide opportunities for the communication of ideas, moods and feelings through the expressive use of the body. Literature, too, has much in common with dance in its use of imagery and rhythmic patterns. Gymnastics is also dependent on the rhythmic use of the body, not only for the efficient and economical performance of skills, but also to add interest to the sequences made by the children.

Through gymnastics and dance children can be helped to understand concepts of shape and space. They can physically experience what it means to be 'on', 'under', 'over', 'in front', 'behind'. They can move backwards, forwards, on the diagonal, sideways, in linear or curving pathways. They can experience rotation, symmetry and asymmetry in a practical situation. Concepts of force and energy can also be reinforced in a gymnastics or dance situation as can the concepts of matching and mirroring. The children's linguistic ability to describe what they are doing, using both technical and non-technical languages and to express their ideas is also being developed in these situations.

Many of the dance and gymnastics ideas presented in this chapter were either used as starting points for other curriculum areas or were used to extend them. Some ideas for cross-curricular links have therefore been shown for each unit of work.

Work unit: Reception

Aims of unit

To introduce the concepts of:

a Stretching and curling
b Travelling and stillness
c Quick and slow movements.

Objectives	Lesson 1		Lesson 2		Lesson 3		Lesson 4		Lesson 5		Lesson 6	
	Dance	Gym	Dance	Gym	Dance	Gym	Dance	Gym	Dance	Gym	Dance	Gym
To enable the child to show, use and identify the concepts of												
Stretching and curling	☑	☑	✓	☑	✓	☑	✓	☑	✓	✓	✓	✓
Making wide stretched shapes	✓		✓	✓		✓		✓				✓
Making curled rounded shapes	☑	☑	✓	✓	✓	✓	✓	✓		✓		✓
Making spiky body shapes				☑	☑		☑					
Travelling, to include galloping	✓		✓									
Travelling, to include marching	✓		✓									
Travelling, to include skips/hops/bounces		✓		✓				✓	☑	✓	✓	
Freezing movement		✓			☑	✓	☑					
Quick and slow movements								✓	☑	☑	✓	☑
Strong movements					☑	✓	☑					

Key: ☑ a main emphasis in the lesson ✓ an emphasis in the lesson

All three aspects of each activity, i.e. composing, performing and appreciating in dance, and planning, performing and evaluating in gymnastics, should be apparent in every lesson.

Assessment

This should relate directly to the overall aims of the unit and the specific objectives for each lesson.

Dances within unit

Lessons 1–2		Humpty Dumpty
♪	Accompaniment:	No 1 on the cassette
	Resources:	An egg
Lessons 3–4		Where the Wild Things Are
♪	Accompaniment:	No 2 on the cassette
	Resources:	'Where the Wild Things Are' by Maurice Sendak (Puffin, 1970)
Lessons 5–6		Winnie the Pooh
♪	Accompaniment:	No 3 on the cassette
	Resources:	Winnie the Pooh puppet

Gymnastics within unit

Lessons 1–6   Stretching and curling

Reception: cross-curricular links

Science

- Describe what a raw egg looks like. How does it move? What do fried, boiled and scrambled eggs look like? How do they move? Establish the permanent change of state of cooked eggs.
- Make egg sandwiches. Establish the hygiene 'rules' needed to do this. Taste the difference that salt, pepper and mayonnaise make to the sandwich.
- Incubate eggs and watch the chicks hatch. Consider the need for warmth and careful handling of the chicks.
- Look at and describe the difference between thick and thin honey. Which falls faster when dropped from a warm spoon on to a plate?
- Look at and feel objects that are smooth, rough or spiky.
- Name parts of animals, e.g. eyes, tails, paws, whiskers.

Humpty Dumpty

Winnie the Pooh

Mathematics

- Classify and sort animals and birds into sets according to either colour, pattern, whether or not they have tails, wings, fur or feathers and whether they fly, jump or run.

English

- Read *Meg's Eggs* by Helen Nicoll and Jan Pienkowski (Puffin).
- Learn and say nursery rhymes.
- Describe a pet.

Music

- Show pictures of animals. Talk about and make the sound that the animal makes.
- Sequence the pictures to make sound compositions. Explore the use of percussion intruments to match vocal sounds.

Art

- Draw pictures of the 'Wild Things'.
- Paint egg shells. Break them into small pieces and use the pieces to make a Humpty Dumpty picture.

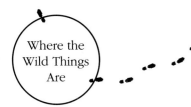

Where the Wild Things Are

Humpty Dumpty

Dance Framework

1 Begin curled up and grow into a wide, spread shape.
2 Collapse into a jagged shape.
3 Gallop.
4 March and salute.

Lesson 1

A Introduction

1 Ask the class to sit close to you. 'Watch my hands and copy what I do.' Open and close your hands, sometimes both at the same time, sometimes one after the other, using quick and slow movements. Sometimes spread all your fingers at the same time and sometimes one after the other. Make this into a game-like activity. Ask the children to describe the shape that their hands have made, i.e. curled up and stretched.

2 'Show me, with your weight on your feet, how you can make your whole body into a curled shape. Tuck your head well in and make your back as rounded as possible. Now slowly stretch up as tall as you can to the ceiling. Imagine your fingers and your nose are attached by strings to the ceiling. Suddenly collapse down to your curled shape again.'

Practise several times.

'Grow into a wide spread shape.'

B Movement exploration and development

1 'Gallop anywhere in the room, using all the space.' Give the imagery of horses. 'Show me how you hold the reins of your horse as it gallops.'

2 'Let's march on the spot. Show me how high you can get your knees.' Give the imagery of marching. 'Now march anywhere in the room.'

3 'Do you know a nursery rhyme in which soldiers march and horses gallop and someone falls over?'

Say the rhyme of 'Humpty Dumpty' with the class. Listen to the music and relate the rhyme to the music and to the dance idea, as in the framework.

4 'Let's curl up small and grow as wide and as big as Humpty Dumpty. Suddenly he falls off the wall.' Everyone collapses to the floor.

5 'Here come the king's horses. Show me how you can gallop without touching anyone.'

6 'Now here come the king's men marching. Let's salute at the end.'

C Dance

1 Slowly grow into a wide shape.

2 Collapse down to the floor.

3 Gallop.

4 March and salute.

D Conclusion

'Curl up tightly and tiptoe to the door when I touch you.'

Reception

Lesson 2

Humpty Dumpty

Lesson 2

A Introduction

Repeat the introduction to Lesson 1.

B Movement exploration and development

1 'Let's practise galloping again. Gallop towards me, then away from me.'

2 'Let's try marching. Remember to lift your knees up high and swing your arms.'

3 'Come and sit near me.' Show the children a broken egg shell. 'What do the edges of the shell look like?'

Encourage the use of words such as pointed, sharp and spiky.

Ask the children to show you:

a spiky fingers

b spiky knees

c spiky elbows.

'Make your whole body spiky. Lie on your back and make spiky shapes with your arms and legs in the air. See if you can lie on your side or on your front and still make spiky shapes with your arms and legs.'

4 'Let's practise growing into a wide shape and collapsing down into a spiky shape on the floor.'

C Dance

Practise this as outlined in the framework.

D Conclusion

Repeat the conclusion to Lesson 1.

Where the Wild Things Are

Before the lesson, prepare the children by reading *Where the Wild Things Are* by Maurice Sendak. Use pictures from the book as a further stimulus for the dance.

Dance framework

1 From a curled position on the floor, stretch to finish in a spiky shape.

2 Three spiky, sudden jumps on the spot.

3 Run and freeze in a spiky shape. Repeat.

4 Run back to the teacher and freeze.

5 Sink back down to the floor.

Reception

Lesson 3

Where the Wild Things Are

Lesson 3

A Introduction

1 'Run anywhere in the room and freeze your movement when I hit the tambourine.' Repeat several times. 'Pull in your tummies when you stop. Nothing should be moving, not even your eyelashes.'

'Run back towards me and freeze.'

B Movement exploration and development

1 'What do the Wild Things look like? Yes, they are very big. They look very angry and they have very sharp claws.'

'Show me what their claws look like. Yes, they are sharp and pointed, like the egg shell we saw last time.'

2 'Make fists with your hands and show me your muscles. Grip and relax.' Practise several times.

3 'Show me how you can grip the floor with your feet. Make your whole body feel tight. Grip and relax.'

'Show me how strong your whole body is.' Encourage strong arms, legs and middles.

4 'Show me how strong and angry you are as you shoot out your claws.'

5 'Run into a space and freeze into your angry shape, showing your spiky claws.' Practise several times.

6 'Perhaps you could show me a small jump before you freeze.'

7 'Come back to me.'

'When Max comes to the island all the Wild Things are asleep. Curl up on the floor. Show me how you can do an enormous yawn. See if the yawn can lift you on to your feet.' Practise several times.

C Dance

'Let's make a dance.'

1 'Start curled up. Yawn and yawn and yawn on to your feet.'

2 'Run and freeze into a spiky shape.' Repeat three times.

3 'Slowly, slowly sink to the floor.'

D Conclusion

Look at some of the dances. Who has spiky fingers? Who looks very angry?

Lesson 4
Reception
4
Where the Wild Things Are

Lesson 4

A Introduction

1 'Curl up on the floor and stretch to stand.'

2 'Show me your spiky fingers. Curl up your fists, then shoot out your fingers.'

3 'Curl up tightly. Yawn and yawn and yawn until you are standing up. Show your claws.'

B Movement exploration and development

1 'Show me your angry, spiky shape. Jump into another one and another and another.'

'Sometimes make your "claws" go high and sometimes make them low down.' (Demonstrations may be needed here.)

2 'Let's practise running and freezing into a spiky shape.' Repeat several times.

3 'Max told the Wild things to be still and they were, so run back to me and freeze.'

4 'Gently sink back down to sleep.'

C Dance

Practise as outlined in the framework.

D Conclusion

Look at the dances and comment on them.

Winnie the Pooh

The stimulus for this dance is a Winnie the Pooh rod puppet.

Dance framework

1 Rise up slowly into a tall shape and sink down quickly. Repeat.

2 Jump up suddenly.

3 Travel with skips, hops and bounces.

4 Jump down to the floor to finish in a curled shape.

Reception

Lesson 5

Winnie the Pooh

Lesson 5

A Introduction

1 'Bounce and jump and hop and skip anywhere in the room.' Encourage as much variety as possible.

B Movement exploration and development

1 'Come and sit close to me.' Show how the Winnie the Pooh puppet appears out of his honey pot. You can make him rise up quickly and sink down slowly or vice versa. Decide on your pattern. For example, rise up slowly, disappear down quickly and rise up quickly.

2 'Let's stretch up slowly like Winnie the Pooh. Make yourself as tall as you can. Shoot down quickly.' Practise several times.

3 'Show me how you can jump up out of your honey pot.'

4 'Let's practise rising up slowly, sinking down quickly and jumping up suddenly.'

C Dance

'In our dance, Winnie the Pooh escapes from the honey pot. Show how he might travel to find another one.' Remind the children of the bounces, hops and jumps they did at the beginning of the lesson. 'Find another honey pot and jump down into it.'

Practise the whole dance, as outlined in the framework.

D Conclusion

Look at the dances and comment.

Reception

Lesson 6

Winnie the Pooh

Lesson 6

This could be almost the same as Lesson 5, but you could vary the speed and the number of times that Winnie the Pooh emerges from and disappears into the honey pot. You could also introduce the idea of turning, e.g. 'Jump up quickly and sink down slowly, turning as you go. Repeat, then jump up quickly.'

Reception:
Lesson plans for gymnastics

Stretching and curling

Lesson 1

A Warm-up

1 'Run in and out of each other, and when I say "Stop" can you stand still, like statues?' Repeat several times.

2 'Run in and out of each other, and when I say "Stop" can you sit down on the floor?' Repeat several times.

3 'Run in and out of each other, and instead of saying "Stop" I will call "Sit" or "Stand" or "Lie down".' Repeat several times in different order.

5 'Run around the hall, anywhere you like, but not in a circle – find spaces to run into.' Play a game of 'Go' and 'Freeze' and when they freeze check that they are in a good space. Emphasise running quietly.

B Floorwork

1 'Can you bend down low on your feet and make a very tight ball? Remember to tuck your head and elbows in, and pull your arms tightly round your knees.'

2 'Is there any other way you can curl up tightly in a ball on the floor?' Show the different body parts that can be on the floor when they are curled up – back, side, knees, shoulders, bottom. Let the children experience all these different ways.

3 'Can you stretch up as high as possible? Show me strong bodies, stretched fingers and feet. Reach for the ceiling.'

4 'Curl up on your feet again. Can you stay curled up and travel to another place in the hall?' Show some examples and let everyone try out the ideas.

C Apparatus

1 Take out benches and low tables. 'Can you run in and out of the apparatus without touching it?'

2 'Can you travel in and out and underneath the apparatus when it is clear? Can you keep moving and not bump into anyone?'

3 'Can you travel in and out, under and over your apparatus, never standing still?'

4 'Can you travel over/under/around your apparatus and find places where you can curl up?'

5 'Can you travel over/under/around your apparatus and find places where you can stretch out?'

D Calming-down activity

'Hold hands with a friend and walk, then trot, in and out of each other in pairs.'

Lesson 2

A Warm-up

1 'Run in and out of each other and into spaces. Stop when I clap my hands.' Repeat several times.

2 'Run and when you stop this time, see how small you can be.'

3 'Run and, this time, see how tall you can be.' You could use a tambourine to make a game of this, e.g. two taps for becoming small and one tap for tall.

B Floorwork

1 'Run, stop and see how small you can be. Can you remember the different parts you can curl up on?' Feet/side/back/bottom/shoulders/knees – ask children to try all these parts.

2 'Can you travel slowly and carefully to another spot keeping as small as possible?' You could demonstrate travelling on knees, rolling over sideways and back on to knees again; taking tiny footsteps. Let all the children try out these ideas.

3 'Can you stretch up high?' Remind them of tension in body and to stretch fingers and toes.

4 'Can you travel to another place in the hall in a very stretched-out way?' Choose several of the children's ideas and let everyone try them.

C Apparatus

1 'Can you go over/under/around your apparatus and use the floor? Explore.'

2 'Can you find a place on your apparatus where you can curl up? When you have done this, go to another part of the apparatus and curl up.' Repeat several times.

3 'Can you travel on the floor or over/under your apparatus in a stretched or a curled way?' Choose some of the children's ideas and let everyone try them.

D Calming-down activity

'Practise a favourite movement.'

Lesson 3

A Warm-up

1 'Can you travel in and out of each other and into spaces? Stop.' Repeat several times.

2 'Travel in and out of each other and into spaces – Stop – make a small shape.' Repeat several times.

3 Repeat 2 but, when the children have stopped in a small curled position, ask them to 'slowly grow up tall and thin, with stretched fingers and toes'. Repeat several times.

B Floorwork

1 Curl up tightly – head in, knees bent, elbows in. Can you remember the different parts that we can be small on?' Backs/sides/knees/feet/shoulders.

2 'Travel slowly in a small curled-up position. Can you move in different directions when you are curled up on your feet?

3 'Stretch out as tall or as wide as possible. Keep tight, strong bodies, stretched fingers and toes. Can you move to another space in a stretched-out shape?

4 'Do we always have to be stretched out standing up? What other stretched positions can you find?' Show examples and then let children try again.

C Apparatus

1 'Travel over/under/around your apparatus. Explore it.'

2 'Travel over/under/around/your apparatus and find places where you can stretch.' Show some examples and establish if positions are wide/thin/high/low. Repeat the task.

3 'Can you travel on the floor and over/under your apparatus sometimes curled and sometimes stretched?'

'Find places where you can stretch out.'

D Calming-down activity

'Bounce around the hall forwards, sideways and backwards.'

Reception

Lesson **4**

Stretching and curling

Lesson 4

A Warm-up

1 'Can you run in and out of each other and stop, making a tall shape if I beat the tambourine once and making a small shape if I beat twice?' Repeat several times – reminding them each time of the small and tall shapes they can make.

2 'On a beat of the tambourine, make a small curled shape and then, on a shake of the tambourine, grow slowly into a stretched shape.'

Remind them about stretched shapes being possible in different ways and on different levels. Repeat several times.

B Floorwork

1 'Can you move carefully and slowly about the hall in a curled-up position and then, when I shake the tambourine, grow slowly into a stretched position?' Repeat several times. 'Remember you can be stretched and thin, stretched and wide and stretched on different levels.' Demonstrate ways of being stretched on different levels and let everyone try out the ideas.

2 'Can you move about the hall in a bouncy, energetic way and, when I say "Stop", curl up tightly?'

3 'Can you move about the hall in a stretched-out position and, when I say "Stop", curl up quickly?'

C Apparatus

1 'Travel over/under/around your apparatus. Explore it.'

2 'Show ways of travelling on your apparatus and mat. Sometimes you should be stretched and sometimes curled.'

3 'Can you find a piece of apparatus to curl up on and then slowly grow into a stretched shape?' Show some examples and let everyone try the different ideas.

D Calming-down activity

'Move around the hall as lightly as possible.'

Reception

Lesson 5

Stretching and curling

Lesson 5

A Warm-up

1 Play a game of crossing signals. 'When I say "Green man", you must run and, when I say "Red man", you must stop.' Repeat this several times.

2 'Let's play the game again but, this time, on green, can you walk or bounce as close to the ground as possible and, on red, can you stop, curled up very small?'

B Floorwork

1 'Can you move about the hall, sometimes in a stretched-out way and sometimes in a curled-up way?'

2 'Can you move around the hall in a bouncy, energetic way and, when I say "Stop", curl up tightly?' Demonstrate and repeat.

3 'Move around the hall in a bouncy, energetic way and, when I say "Stop", curl up tightly and then open up slowly into a stretched position.' Repeat several times and remind children about different levels for stretching.

C Apparatus

1 'Can you travel over/under/around your apparatus? Explore it.'

2 'Can you move over/under/around your apparatus, sometimes in a curled way and sometimes in a stretched way?'

3 'Can you move stretched on to a piece of apparatus and come down to the ground curled?'

D Calming-down activity

'Hold hands with a partner and walk in and out of each other.'

Lesson 6

A Warm-up

1 'Can you remember the crossing-man game from last lesson? When I say "Green man" you run and when I say "Red man" you stop.'

2 'Now when I say "Green man" can you curl up and bounce close to the ground? When I call out "Red man" can you stop in a stretched shape?'

3 'When I say "Green man" can you bounce in a stretched-out way two feet to two feet? When I call out "Red man" you must stop in a stretched shape.'

B Floorwork

1 'Can you travel round the hall in a stretched-out fast way?'

2 'Can you travel round the hall in a stretched-out slow way?' Show some examples and let everyone try the ideas.

3 'Can you travel round the hall in a curled-up slow way?' Show some examples and let everyone try.

4 'Can you travel round the room sometimes in a stretched-out fast way and sometimes in a curled-up slow way?'

5 'Travel round the hall, sometimes stretched, sometimes curled, sometimes slow and sometimes fast. I need to be able to see what you are doing.'

C Apparatus

1 'Travel under/over and in and out of the apparatus, sometimes making your body large, sometimes small, sometimes moving quickly and sometimes slowly.'

2 'Travel in the same way but, when you come to a piece of apparatus, can you stop on it still as a statue, sometimes stretched out, sometimes curled up? Count 1, 2, 3, and then ask children to travel to another piece of apparatus.

D Calming-down activity

'Sit in a curled position and then stand up showing a good stretched position.'

Aims of unit

1 To increase awareness of:

  a Body shape
  b Dynamics
  c Levels.

2 To introduce the concept of linear and curved floor pathways.

Objectives	Lesson 1		Lesson 2		Lesson 3		Lesson 4		Lesson 5		Lesson 6	
	Dance	Gym	Dance	Gym	Dance	Gym	Dance	Gym	Dance	Gym	Dance	Gym
To enable the child to show, use and identify												
Rhythmic responses	☑		☑									
Curled and stretched shapes	✓	✓	✓	✓		✓		☑	☑	✓	☑	✓
Spiky/narrow/wide shapes		☑		☑	✓	✓	✓					✓
Sudden, sharp movements			✓	☑	✓	✓	✓					
Sustained, smooth movements						✓	✓	☑		☑		☑
Freezing movements	✓	✓						✓	✓		✓	
Curved floor pathways								✓	☑	✓	☑	✓
Linear and angular floor pathways										☑		☑
High/low movements	✓		✓	✓	✓	✓	✓	✓	✓	✓	✓	✓
Jumping				✓		☑				✓		✓

Key: ☑ a main emphasis in the lesson   ✓ an emphasis in the lesson

All three aspects of each activity, i.e. composing, performing and appreciating in dance, and planning, performing and evaluating in gymnastics, should be apparent in every lesson.

Assessment

This should relate directly to the overall aims of the unit and the specific objectives for each lesson.

Dances within unit

♪ **Lessons 1–2**   Rain
  Accompaniment: Voice, tambourine and woodblock
  Resources: *Rain* by K. Taniuchi and P. Blakeley (A & C Black, 1980)
♪ **Lessons 3–4**   Jack Frost
  Accompaniment: No 4 on the cassette
♪ *Resources:* Pictures of frost
Lessons 5–6   Coming to school
  Accompaniment: No 5 on the cassette
  Resources: None required

Gymnastics within unit

Lessons 1–6   Wide / Narrow / curled

Year 1: cross-curricular links

Geography

- Weather charts – children use own observations to construct weather charts making their own symbols.
- Make rain gauges.
- Draw simple maps created by the pathways used in the dance.
- Make symbols to indicate shops or houses along the route.
- Describe ways in which people make journeys.
- Give reasons why people make journeys of different lengths.

Coming to school

Art

- Make rain pictures inspired by the illustrations in the book. Use wet paint for the background and paint in details when the background is dry.
- Look at patterns of frost on windows. Describe and draw these on black paper.

Rain/ Jack Frost

Mathematics

- Make block charts to show modes of transport to school.

History

- Look at pictures to show how homes and modes of transport have changed through time.

Science/mathematics

- Collect rain in a clear container. Measure the depth. Freeze the water collected, then measure the depth again. Record the results.

Music

- Explore and use a range of sounds made by the voice and body inspired by **a** the rain **b** different modes of transport.
- Create a musical pattern to match a movement pattern inspired by the rain or Jack Frost.

English

- Find rain and weather rhymes.
- Use onomatopoeic words to describe the sounds that rain makes.
- Use these to make a poem. Listen and describe the sound that rain makes on different surfaces, e.g. an umbrella, the roof, a window. Use these to make a poem.
- Describe an imaginary journey.

Science

- Why do we need rain? What would happen if it did not rain?
- Heating and cooling water. Make ice lollies. What happens when you leave them out of the freezer? How long do they take to melt?
- How long do they take to freeze? What conditions aid freezing and melting?

'A map to show the way from my house to school.'

Year 1:
Lesson plans for dance _____

Rain

The original stimulus for this dance was *Rain* by K. Taniuchi and P. Blakeley. However, it is not essential to have read the book in order to use the idea of rain as a starting point for this dance.

Dance framework

1 Rhythmic pattern beating fingers on the floor, finishing with a jump into the air.

2 Run and curl up close to the floor. Run and stretch high. Repeat.

3 Gradual sinking to the floor with staccato movements.

4 Own ending, e.g. flat shape or roll and stop.

Year 1

Lesson 1

Rain

Lesson 1

A Introduction

1 'Show me how tall you can be. Stretch as high as you can. Now curl up very small. Remember to tuck your head in, but keep your weight on your feet.' Repeat several times.

B Movement exploration and development

1 'Run into a space and stop when I hit the tambourine.' Give coaching points for stopping suddenly, i.e. 'Pull in your tummies and grip the floor with your feet.'

2 'This time, when you stop, freeze in your curled shape.' Practise this.

3 'Run and stop in your tall shape.'

4 'This time we will play a game. If you have to finish in a tall shape I will hit the tambourine twice. If you have to finish in a curled shape I will only hit it once.' By making this a game-like activity you will be able to practise these movements for a longer period of time to improve the quality of the sudden stopping and of the curled and tall shapes.

5 The children will already have listened to the story in the classroom, but show them again the pictures of children running through the rain. Ask the children how the boys ran for cover in the story and remind them of the curled shapes they might have to make to shelter from the rain. Remind them how they might stretch up tall to see if it is still raining.

If you have not read the book with the children, ask them to imagine sheltering from the rain – curled shapes – and then stretching up tall to check if it is still raining.

6 Put together the phrase of running and curling up small and running and stretching tall. Repeat the phrase several times, then slowly sink down to the floor.

7 Discuss the noise the rain makes on the pavement or on a roof. 'Tap your

fingers on the floor so that they sound like rain.' Discuss words which describe the sound of the rain. For example, 'pitter patter, split, splat, splot, drip, drop, plip, plop'.

Use voices to create rhythmic patterns, e.g. pitter, patter, pit: split, splat, splot. You could beat these one at a time on the floor while the children listen. They then beat the same pattern back. Decide on one simple pattern (e.g. pitter, patter, pit), perhaps repeated three times.

8 Remind the children how the rain sometimes comes down so heavily that it rebounds from the pavement. Practise tapping the rhythm with fingers on the floor and then jumping up suddenly into the air.

9 Practise the rhythm of:

Pitter, patter, pit

Pitter, patter, pit

Pitter, patter, PIT (explode into the air with a jump on the final 'pit').

C Dance

Dance 1 and 2 of the rain framework.

D Conclusion

'Curl up very small. When I touch you on the shoulder, tiptoe quietly to the door.'

Lesson 2

A Introduction

1 'Shake your hands/one leg/the other leg/all over.'

2 'Let's practise the dance we made last week.' Recap this with the children.

B Movement exploration and development

Discuss the way that raindrops fall off the leaves on the trees after the rain has stopped. Discuss words to describe this, e.g. drip drop or plip plop.

1 'Stretch up tall and show me how the raindrops fall to the ground.' Use your voice and a two-tone wood block to encourage sudden staccato movements from the children as they sink to the ground. Practise several times, improving on the suddenness and sharpness of movements.

2 Ask the children what might happen to the raindrops, e.g. they might form puddles or they might roll away slowly into the gutter and down the drain 'Show me how you are going to end your dance.'

C Dance

Practise the whole dance.

D Conclusion

Stand up slowly, stretch high, then return to a 'good' standing position.

Jack Frost

Dance framework

1 Grow into a spiky shape.

2 Four small jumps into four different spiky shapes using changes of level.

3 Skip with spiky knees, elbows and fingers. Freeze.

4 Melt into any shape.

Year 1

Lesson 3

Jack Frost

Lesson 3

A Introduction

1 Ask the class to sit close to you.'Show me how spiky you can make your fingers. Show me how spiky you can make your elbows.'

2 'Move your hands and elbows smoothly and then freeze into spiky shapes.' Repeat this several times.

Spiky fingers, spiky feet.

B Movement exploration and development

1 'Move into a space. Show me how your fingers can shoot into the space all around you.' Encourage sudden, staccato movements and the use of different levels.

2 'Skip anywhere in the room. Now show me how you can skip, making your knees spiky and sharp. Imagine that you are bursting balloons with your spiky knees.'

3 'This time let me see you skipping with spiky knees and darting spiky fingers. Imagine Jack Frost turning everything he touches to ice.'

4 'As I play the tambourine, show me your spiky skipping movements and, each time the music stops, freeze in a spiky shape.' Show some examples.

5 'Jump towards me with a spiky shape, and again, and again. Slowly melt.'

6 'Let's practise curling up small and growing slowly into a spiky shape.'

C Dance

'Grow slowly into a spiky shape then skip with spiky knees and fingers and freeze. Melt.'

D Conclusion

'As I touch you, tiptoe to the door.'

Year 1

Lesson

4

Jack Frost

Lesson 4

A Introduction

1 Spiky skipping anywhere in the hall.

2 'Skip back to me and melt until you are sitting down.'

B Movement exploration and development

1 'Curl up and grow slowly into a spiky shape.'

2 'See how smoothly you can grow, then freeze very suddenly. Hold your spiky shape, then jump into another one, and again, and again.' Emphasise the angularity of the shapes and the suddenness of the small jumps.

3 'Show me one of your spiky shapes. Make your hands and fingers as obvious as possible. Can you make one of your hands go high with the other one going low? Change over the position of your hands. See if you can remember some of these positions as you jump into your shapes.'

   'Let's practise these four small sudden jumps which make you change your shape each time.' Emphasise different levels, not only of the hands but of the whole body.

4 'Let's practise melting again. Show me how smoothly and softly you can do this. What sort of shape do you finish in? Is it rounded or spiky or flat?'

C Dance

Practise the dance according to the framework.

D Conclusion

Show some of the dances and comment on them. Ask for the children's comments.

Coming to school

Dance framework

1 Beginning in a curled shape, stretch into a wide shape and return suddenly to a curled shape. Repeat three more times, taking weight on different body parts at different levels.

2 Skip using own chosen pathway.

Year 1

Lesson **5**

Coming to school

Lesson 5

A Introduction

1 Ask class to sit close to you. 'Curl and stretch your hands and fingers.'
(Repeat introduction to Rain, Lesson 1.)

B Movement exploration and development

1 'Stretch your whole body into a wide shape.' Look at some examples, e.g. some children may be stretching one arm high and the other one low; some may stretch out on the floor.

2 'Stretch into a wide shape, STR-E-TCH and collapse!'

3 'Practise curling up quickly. How quietly can you do it?'

4 'Skip anywhere in the hall. Remember to point your knees up to the ceiling and your toes down to the ground.' Practise skipping on the spot to emphasise pointed knees and toes, then skip in and out and round about.

5 Talk about the idea of waking up and coming to school. Relate the movements already done to the dance idea, i.e. stretching and yawning into a wide shape; then diving back into bed in a curled shape; finally skipping to school.

6 'Let's practise yawning and stretching and diving back into bed. In our dance we will do this four times.'

7 'Let's do that again and go straight into the skipping.'

8 Discuss with the children the route that they take to school. Do they go around corners or roundabouts? Do they cross bridges or meet traffic lights?

'Show me what happens when you come to a roundabout.' Emphasise skipping in circles.

'Show me what happens when you come to a corner.' Encourage an angular floor pathway. Demonstrations from the children may be needed here.

'In the skipping section, you must go around at least one corner and one roundabout.'

C Dance

Practise the dance made so far.

D Conclusion

'Stand "well" and tiptoe to the door.'
Before the next lesson, ask children to draw their route to school.

Year 1

Lesson **6**

Coming to school

Lesson 6

A Introduction

1 'Skip on a journey around the room. Remember to go around corners and roundabouts and then skip back to me.'

2 Discuss the routes that the children have drawn. Look at some of the individual routes. 'How many corners are there on this route? Let's practise skipping around the three corners on this map.'

B Movement exploration and development

1 'What happens if the traffic lights are red when you come to them? Let's practise skipping, slowing down and skipping on the spot at the traffic lights before skipping off again.'

2 'How might we show going over the bridge? Yes, you could jump.'

3 'Skip your own route to school.'

4 'Some people do not come very far so perhaps everyone could pretend to go around at least one roundabout and one corner. You can include the traffic lights and bridges if you wish.'

5 'Let's practise the yawns and stretches again. Practise stretching and coming up on to your feet. Perhaps you could try balancing on one foot instead of both feet. Remember to pull in your tummies so that you can balance more easily.'

'Instead of yawning with your arms, you could try making your legs "yawn", or one arm and one leg "yawn". You could be on your side to yawn, or perhaps you could balance on one knee and two hands.' Encourage some low positions and some high ones.

'Choose your four favourite "yawns". You must include at least one which takes you high and one which takes you low down, close to the floor.'

'Let's practise together your yawns and diving back into bed, finishing in a curled shape.'

C Dance

Practise the whole dance.

D Conclusion

Show some of the dances and encourage discussion and comments.

Year 1:
Lesson plans for gymnastics———

Wide/narrow/curled body shapes

Year 1

Lesson **1**

Wide/narrow/curled

Lesson 1

A Warm-up

1 'Run in and out of each other without making contact. When I call "Stop", freeze very still in a space of your own.'

2 'Run in and out of each other with your hands on your heads.'

3 'Run in and out of each other with your arms tightly by your sides.'

4 'Run in and out of each other with your hands on your hips.' Repeat 1. 'Which was the easiest sort of running? *No 1.* 'What sort of shape were we running in?' *Narrow.*

5 'Run in and out of each other and stop. What shape are you in when you stop?' *Wide.*

B Floorwork

1 'Move around the hall making as many different shapes as you can.' Pick out and show a narrow shape, then ask everyone to try it. 'How can we make it longer?' *With stretched fingers and toes.*

2 'Make as many different long narrow shapes as possible - don't forget you can take your weight on different body parts to produce the shape you want - back/side/front/shoulders and so on.' Demonstrate examples and let the children have another turn. Emphasise tension and strength in the body.

3 'Can you travel making your body long and thin?' Choose some different examples of long, thin shapes and let everyone try the ideas.

4 'What other stretched shape can we make? (Pause) Wide and stretched.' Try out ideas for wide stretched shapes. Remind the children that they do not have to stay on their feet.

5 'Can you travel about the hall making a wide and stretched shape?'

C Apparatus

1 'Travel over/under/around your apparatus. Explore it.'

2 'Travel over/under/around your apparatus. Think about whether you are in a long narrow shape or a wide stretched shape.'

3 'Travel around/under/over your apparatus and, when you come to a clear space, make a wide or narrow stretched position on it and then move on.'

D Calming-down activity

'Move about the hall in as many different ways as possible.'

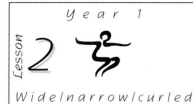

Year 1

Lesson

2

Wide/narrow/curled

Lesson 2

A Warm-up

1 'Run in and out of each other without touching and jump high into the air to make a wide shape.' Show some star jumps and let everyone try them out - take off from two feet.

2 'Can you run in and out of each other and jump to make a long narrow shape in the air?' Show some straight jumps and let everyone try them out - take off from two feet.

B Floorwork

1 'Run in and out of each other into a space and make a wide, short shape.' Repeat several times. Choose some of the children's ideas and let everyone try them.

2 'Run in and out of each other into a space and make a long narrow shape.' Repeat several times. Choose some of the children's ideas and let everyone try them out.

3 'Can you make a long thin shape or a wide short shape with your bottom or feet higher than your head?' Show some examples and then try again.

4 'Can you travel making a long and thin shape into one space, then travel in a wide and short shape into another?'

5 'We've made some tall and wide shapes. What other shape could we make? (Pause) Small and curled. Show me some small curled shapes.' Demonstrate showing different ways of being small and curled on back/knees/side/bottom/feet. Repeat the task.

6 'Can you travel to another part of the room keeping small and tightly curled?'

C Apparatus

1 'Travel/over/under/around your apparatus. Explore it.'

2 'Travel over/under/around your apparatus. Think about making narrow/wide/curled shapes.'

3 'Travel over/under/around your apparatus. Pause on your apparatus in a narrow/wide/curled shape and move on again.'

D Calming-down activity

'Travel sometimes very close to the floor and sometimes tall in the air.'

Year 1

Lesson

3

Wide/narrow/curled

Lesson 3

A Warm-up

Ask children to respond to quick commands of 'Stand up', 'Sit down', 'Kneel down', 'Lie down', 'Sit', 'Lie on side', 'Lie on back', etc. Make this a game.

B Floorwork

1 'Lie down on the floor. Can you show me a wide shape, a narrow shape or a curled shape which is close to the floor?' Look at the different ideas and let everyone try them out.

2 'Can you now show me wide, narrow or curled shapes which are not close to the floor?' Look at all the ideas which are produced and ask everyone to try them out.

3 Ask children to run and jump to show narrow or wide jumps in the air. Remind them that it is easier to take off and land on two feet; to keep up their heads; to use arms to aid flight into the air; to allow ankles/knees/hips to 'give' on landing. Demonstrate.

4 'Sit on the floor, knees bent up, back straight, heads up - this is the shape in the air for a curled jump. Try on the spot first - keep head up, back straight and bring knees up in front.' *Warn children they must keep their heads up or they will rotate forwards.*

5 Determine that it is possible to produce shapes in the air as well as on the ground - can they now run and jump into a space making any shape and then make a shape on the ground? Repeat several times. Remind them about 'give' and 'sinking down' before going into a shape on the ground.

C Apparatus

1 'Travel over/under/around the apparatus. Explore.'

2 'Travel over/under and around the apparatus and, when it is clear, can you jump from a low piece of apparatus in a wide/narrow jump - land and sink down moving into a curled shape?

D Calming-down activity

'Find several different ways of walking.'

Lesson 4

A Warm-up

1 'Run in and out of each other – freeze when I say "Stop".' Repeat this several times.

2 'Bounce in and out of each other. Remember you can bounce in different directions – forwards, backwards and sideways.'

3 'Squat down low. Can you bounce in and out of each other in this low position? Remember to keep bouncing into spaces.'

B Floorwork

1 'Travel round the floor on your hands and feet.' Demonstrate with feet apart - wide shape; feet together and legs straight – narrow shape; feet together and knees bent – small curled shape. Repeat the task and try all the different shapes.

2 'Make a small curled shape - can you roll in that shape?' Demonstrate rolling sideways and let everyone try again.

3 'Run into a space to jump showing a wide/narrow shape, then sink down low to make a small curled shape.' Remind children about 'give' in ankles/hips and knees - sink carefully into the small shape'. Repeat the task.

4 'Run and jump into a space, sink down into a small curled shape and roll away sideways.' Repeat several times and show some examples.

C Apparatus

1 'Travel over/under/around the apparatus. Explore it.'

2 'Travel over/under/around the apparatus on hands and feet. Think about the shape your body is making.'

3 'Travel round your apparatus – think about your body shape – and, when the apparatus is free, jump from a low piece with a wide or narrow shape. Sink down into a curled shape and roll away sideways.'

D Calming-down activity

'Trot around the hall.'

Year 1

Lesson

5

Wide/narrow/curled

Lesson 5

A Warm-up

1 'Travel round the hall in as many different ways as possible – remember not to bump into anyone. If you are on your feet, remember to travel lightly.'

2 'Travel round the hall close to the floor in different ways – remember the different shapes you can make while you are travelling.'

B Floorwork

1 'Run in and out of each other – jump into a space (wide/narrow shape), sink down into a small curled shape and roll away sideways. Remember to "give" as you sink down.'

2 'Travel into a space using a small and curled shape. Then go into a stretched wide or narrow shape and hold it.' Repeat several times and show examples.

3 'Run and jump into a space – sink down small to roll or travel away, and then hold a stretched position to finish.' Repeat several times and show examples.

C Apparatus

1 'Travel over/under/around the apparatus. Explore it.'

2 'Travel round the apparatus, staying close to it.'

3 'Travel round the apparatus, pushing yourself far away from it.'

4 'Travel round the apparatus and when clear, jump from a low piece of apparatus, sink down on landing into a small curled position to roll away sideways, and then hold a stretched position to finish.'

D Calming-down activity

'Hold hands with a partner and skip around the hall.'

Year 1

Lesson

6

Wide/narrow/curled

Lesson 6

A Warm-up

1 'Run in and out of each other and, when you come to a space, jump high into the air.'

2 'Which shape are you going to show me in the air – wide/narrow/curled? Remember to be careful if you do a curled shape – keep your head up all the time.'

3 'Show me running with three different shapes as you jump into the air.' Choose examples of each shape, then let everyone try the shapes shown.

B Floorwork

1 'Can you remember how we jumped and then landed to sink down into a small, curled shape?' All try it.

2 'Can you run and jump in a wide shape and then sink down and roll away in a long, narrow shape?'

3 'Can you start by rolling in a long and narrow shape and then tuck up and roll sideways making your body tight and curled?'

4 'Can you add that movement to the sequence from last week? Try. Run and jump, sink down and log roll into a curled roll.' Repeat several times so that children remember it.

5 'Now can you add a wide stretched balance on to the end?'

C Apparatus

1 'Travel over/under/along your apparatus. Explore it.'

2 'Travel round your apparatus and, when you come to a clear space, can you jump from it and sink down to log roll away?'

3 'Can you now jump from your apparatus to sink down and log roll away going into a curled sideways roll and finish with a wide stretched balance?'

D Calming-down activity

'In pairs, follow my leader round the hall.'

Work unit: Year 2

Aims of unit

1 To increase awareness of:

  a Dynamics
  b Body shape
  c Floor pathways.

2 To explore some compositional possibilities of working with a partner.

Objectives	Lesson 1		Lesson 2		Lesson 3		Lesson 4		Lesson 5		Lesson 6	
	Dance	Gym	Dance	Gym	Dance	Gym	Dance	Gym	Dance	Gym	Dance	Gym
To enable the child to show, use and identify												
Stretched body shapes	✓		✓			✓		✓	✓	✓		
Angular body shapes					[✓]		✓		✓		✓	
Rounded body shapes	✓		✓			✓	✓	✓	✓	✓	✓	
Curved floor pathways				[✓]		✓		✓		✓		
Linear, angular floor pathways		[✓]		[✓]		✓		✓		✓		
Light movement qualities				✓					[✓]		✓	
Strong movement qualities	[✓]	✓	✓	✓	[✓]		✓					
Relaxed movement qualities								[✓]				
Jumping actions	[✓]		✓		✓	[✓]	✓	✓	[✓]	✓	✓	
Working with a partner								[✓]		[✓]	[✓]	✓

Key: [✓] a main emphasis in the lesson   ✓ an emphasis in the lesson

All three aspects of each activity, i.e. composing, performing and appreciating in dance, and planning, performing and evaluating in gymnastics, should be apparent in every lesson.

Assessment

This should relate directly to the overall aims of the unit and the specific objectives for each lesson.

Dances within unit

Lessons 1–2	Jack-in-the-box
♪ *Accompaniment:*	No 6 on the cassette
Resources:	Jack-in-the-box toy, and/or a spring
Lessons 3–6	Anger, sadness, happiness
♪ *Accompaniment:*	No 7 on the cassette
Resources:	None required

Gymnastics within unit

Lessons 1–4
(although written in four lessons, this unit will take much longer to teach)   Pathways (straight/zigzag/curving)

Year 2: cross-curricular links (Key Stage 1)

English

- Read *Angry Arthur* by H. Oram and S. Kitamura (Puffin, 1984) and use it as a starting point to talk about what makes them and/or other people angry, happy and sad.
- Describe what people look like when they feel these emotions.
- Write poems based on what an emotion feels like, tastes like, looks like, smells like and sounds like (see page 78).

Geography

- *Angry Arthur* could stimulate work on the weather, as Arthur's anger becomes a 'storm cloud exploding thunder, lightning and hailstones'.
- Use words and pictures to describe observations and experiences of the weather.
- Test the force of wind by using streamers made of different materials, e.g. card, plastic and paper.
- Investigate the effects of weather on themselves and their surroundings and recognise seasonal weather patterns.
- Look at and describe how lightning lights up the sky.
- Listen and describe the sound of thunder.

Science

- Describe how a toy with a simple mechanism works.
- Understand that pushing and pulling can make things start to move, speed up and stop.
- Describe what happens when a spring is squashed.

Music

- Explore making vocal and instrumental sounds that describe anger, happiness and sadness.
- Make vocal sounds and/or instrumental sounds which rise and fall.

Art

- Make a picture showing a happy scene, e.g. a birthday party.
- Draw/paint angry, sad and happy faces.

Mathematics

- Understand the notion of angle related to angular shapes.
- Recognise and name shapes, e.g. sphere and cube.

Technology

- Make springs from folded paper.

Angry Arthur by Hiawyn Oram and Satoshi Kitamura

- Anger
- Happiness
- Sadness

Jack-in-the-box (toys)

Sadness

Sadness is like the alphabet
with no letters
Sadness is like I'm stuck in
another dimension.
Sadness is like a dark and
gloomy pit.
Sadness is like a dead flower.
Sadness is a feeling that no-one
likes you.
Sadness feels like someone leaving.
Sadness is like a night sky with
no stars.

Robert

'Sadness' by Robert.

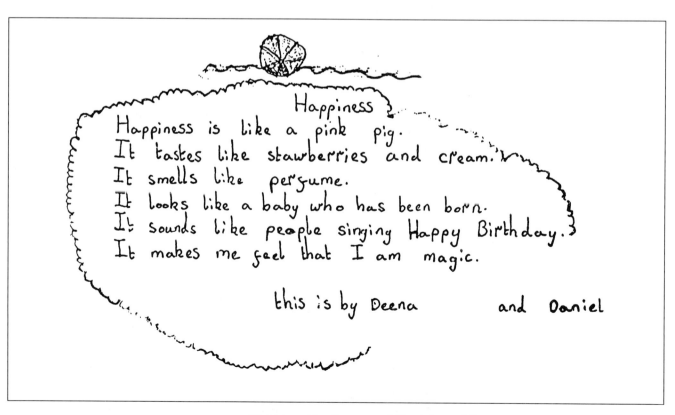

Happiness
Happiness is like a pink pig.
It tastes like stawberries and cream.
It smells like perfume.
It looks like a baby who has been born.
It sounds like people singing Happy Birthday.
It makes me feel that I am magic.

this is by Deena and Daniel

'Happiness' by Deena and Daniel, aged 8 years.

Year 2:
Lesson plans for dance

Jack-in-the-box

Dance framework

1 Wriggling middles, explode into a stretched shape and spiral down to a curled shape. Repeat three times.

2 Own phrase to include:
  a running and jumping into stretched shapes
  b spiralling up and down.

3 Finish in a curled position back in the box.

Year 2

Lesson 1

Jack-in-the-box

Lesson 1

A Introduction

1 'Copy me as I clap my hands and click my fingers. Watch carefully so that you can change when I do.'

2 'See if you can repeat this pattern.' You do eight claps, eight clicks, four claps, four clicks, two claps, two clicks, one clap, one click, one clap, one click.

3 'Bounce on the spot as if your toes are glued to the floor. Let your knees and ankles feel "soft". Now see if you can show me little bounces with your feet coming off the floor.'

4 'Bounce into a space and jog back to me.' Repeat this several times.

B Movement exploration and development

Remind the class of the Jack-in-the-box they have seen in the classroom and establish what a Jack-in-the-box does, i.e. that he shoots up quickly and is pressed back down slowly into his box.

1 'Go into a space and curl up tightly. When I bang the tambour, spring up as fast as you can.' Practise several times. 'Most people are springing on to two feet, perhaps you could try jumping on to one foot.' Encourage suddenness and as high a jump as possible.

2 'What shape does the Jack-in-the-box make in the air? Show me.' To clarify the shape you could ask the children to stand holding their shape without jumping. 'Can you describe your shape? Let's try putting that shape into your jump.'

3 'What does the spring look like that holds the Jack-in-the-box? Show me with your hands.' Establish that it spirals. 'Let's try spiralling from high to low to get back into your box.' Emphasise moving slowly and smoothly to contrast with the suddenness of the jump out of the box.

4 'Let's practise exploding out of the box and spiralling gently down.'

5 'What would happen to Jack if he escaped from the box? How would he feel if he were free? Let's practise running and jumping to fill as much space as you can.'

'Think about the shape you are making in the air.' Encourage tall shapes, wide shapes, symmetric and asymmetric shapes.

6 'Choose three of your favourite jumps and practise them. They can be all the same or each one can be different. You choose.'

7 'Show me your jumps and then spiral down into your box'

C Dance

Remind the children of what they have done so far, i.e. exploding out of their boxes, spiralling back in, running and jumping and spiralling down.

The dance so far could be:

1 'Beginning in a curled position on your feet, explode and spiral down.' Repeat.

2 'Explode once more and this time continue to run and explode into the air to fill as much space as possible. Do this three times then spiral back down into your box.'

Practise at least twice.

D Conclusion

Any relaxation exercise.

Year 2
Lesson 2
2
Jack-in-the-box

Lesson 2

A Introduction

Repeat as Lesson 1.

B Movement exploration and development

Remind the children that the Jack-in-the-box is anchored by its legs to the bottom of the box.

1 'Show me what happens to your body if your feet are stuck to the floor and you want to get away.' Encourage flexible movements with different parts of the body leading, especially hips, knees, elbows and shoulders.

2 'Let's see if you can show me these wriggling movements before you explode into the air, so that you wriggle, explode and spiral down.'

3 'Let's practise your "free" movements – the running and jumping that we did last time.'

4 'Perhaps you could spiral up or down as you are travelling between jumps. Perhaps you might spin on the floor to continue your spiral down.' You could practise this as a class activity. Make sure the children spiral and spin in both clockwise and anti-clockwise directions.

C Dance

Practise and perform the whole dance as outlined in the framework.

D Conclusion

Any relaxation activity.

Anger, sadness and happiness

Dance framework

1 a Stamps and jumps and freeze in a strong 'angry' shape. Repeat.

b Run and jump, finishing in an 'angry' shape. Repeat **a** and **b**.

2 'Sad' shape and roll or transfer weight four times.

3 Small jumps, hops, skips on the spot for 16 beats, then small jumps, hops, skips, travelling and turning for 16 beats.

Year 2

Lesson

3

Anger, sadness and happiness

Lesson 3

A Introduction

1 'Copy me.' You do a sequence of bounces from two feet to two feet using the rhythm of the accompaniment, which will eventually be used for the first section of the dance, i.e. three small bounces and freeze; repeat; seven small bounces and freeze; repeat the whole.

B Movement exploration and development

Ask the children to sit close to you. The subject of emotions will already have been discussed in the classroom with the children being invited to say what makes them feel angry.

1 'Show me angry faces and now angry hands.' Encourage clenched fists and strength in the arms.

'Show me what happens to your middles when you are angry – they get very tight and tense.'

'Show me what happens to your whole bodies when you are angry – everything is tight down to your toes, which are gripping the floor. Look at the angles you are making with your body.'

Producing tension in the body is very tiring, so the above tasks should be done very rhythmically, e.g. grip and grip and grip and release.

2 'Run anywhere in the room and freeze.' Practise this several times encouraging the 'gripping' of the whole body, which will help the children to 'freeze' their movements.

3 'Again run and freeze, but this time finish in an angry shape.' Emphasise the strength and angularity of the body.

4 'Shake out the body and relax.'

5 'How do you know that very small children are angry? They can't talk very well, so what do they do to show they are angry?' Establish that they sometimes jump and stamp their feet. It is also important to establish that you know that your class does not behave in this way.

6 'Show me some strong stamps, but remember to let your feet rebound off the floor so that you do not hurt them. Perhaps you could stamp one foot and then the other. Perhaps you could turn as you stamp. What are your arms doing as you stamp? These should look angry as well. They might be punching into the air.' You might encourage the children to use their own stamping patterns or you might make up some of your own, e.g.

a With weight on the left foot, stamp the right foot three times and freeze

    b Repeat with weight on the right foot

    c Stamp alternate feet around in a small circle.

7 Play with the idea of small jumps – from two feet to two feet. Encourage the use of different directions, i.e. forwards, backwards and sideways.

8 Listen to the first section of the music. Analyse this with the children and clap the rhythm with them.

9 The children return to a space and play with the stamps and jumps to make the first part of their stamping, jumping phrase.

10 'Let's practise the run and freeze again. Now show me a huge strong jump to finish in a strong angular shape.'

C Dance

Recap the dance learned so far, i.e. No 1 of the dance framework.

D Conclusion

1 'How do you feel after you have been angry?' All the children we have taught so far have always said that they feel sorry for their anger.

2 'Let's see the anger melt away as you gradually sink to the floor and rest.'

3 Any relaxation exercise.

Year 2

Lesson 4

Anger, sadness and happiness

Lesson 4

A Introduction

1 'Show me your bounces and stamps sequence that you made last time.'

2 'Show me the run, jump and freeze phrase.'

3 'Put the two phrases together.' You should play the tambour for this, using the same rhythmic sequence as used in the musical accompaniment.

4 'Listen to the music and practise the angry section.' You might still wish to play the tambour while the music is playing to emphasise the rhythm for the children.

B Movement exploration and development

Remind the children of how they feel after they have been angry, i.e. sorry(!) and sad.

1 'Show me a sad face.' The body tends to sink downwards and close into itself. Emphasise this and show some examples.

2 'Show me what you look like when you are sad and lying down.' Encourage different positions with weight on different body parts. Encourage the different relationships to the floor, i.e. facing the floor, with back towards the floor or sideways to the floor.

3 'Show me how sad you look in a sitting position – then when you are standing up. Always emphasise the feeling of being drawn towards the floor.'

4 'Practise moving from standing to sitting to lying as smoothly and as slowly as you can. Feel as if you are melting towards the floor.' Reverse this and come back to standing.

5 'Sit on the floor and see if you can gently spin by pushing yourself round with one hand. Try spinning the other way. See if you can spin and roll sideways into a lying position on your front or back. Can you roll back into a sitting position? See how smoothly and gently you can do this.' Allow plenty of time to practise this.

6 Listen to the second section of the music – point out the smooth quality of the sound and how the music 'says' when to go and when to pause.

7 'Choose four sad shapes. At least one should be standing, one sitting and one lying. Practise smoothly going from one to another.' You will need to accompany this with your voice or using percussion before trying this section with the music.

C Dance

Practise the dance made so far (Nos 1 and 2 of the framework), emphasising the difference in dynamics between the two sections, i.e. the strength and suddenness of the first section and the smoothness and heaviness of the second.

D Conclusion

Listen to the third section of the music and ask the children how it makes them feel? How do they feel when the argument is over and everyone is friendly again? Improvise to music.

Year 2

Lesson 5

Anger, sadness and happiness

Lesson 5

A Introduction

1 Bounces, hops and jumps on the spot. Use all of the five basic jumps.

2 Travel with skips, gallops and hops. Repeat 1 and 2.

B Movement exploration and development

1 Discuss with the class what makes them happy. 'How do you move if you are really happy. Do you jump for joy? Show me what sort of jumps you might use.' Establish the difference between the jumps used to show anger and the ones used to show happiness. The former are stronger and are probably much more earthbound, while the latter are more likely to be lighter, quicker and directed away from the ground.

2 Listen to the third section of the music. There are four counts of eight beats. Beat them with the children. 'For the first 16 beats your movements should be on the spot and, for the last 16, they should travel. Let's try this with the music.'

C Dance

Recap Nos 1 and 2 of the framework. Put the whole dance together. Ask the children to watch each other's dances, but remember to give them specific points to look for.

D Conclusion

Any relaxation exercise.

Year 2

Lesson

6

Anger, sadness and happiness

Lesson 6

A Introduction

Recap the whole dance made in Lessons 3, 4 and 5.

B Movement exploration and development

Discuss with the children if there are any sections of their dances that might work well with a partner. In fact, all of the sections probably would, but in different ways. It is probably a good idea to start with the sad section of the dance, as this is the slowest and will show more easily some of the relationships possible when working with a partner.

1 'I'd like someone to show the class a "sad" shape. Good. Someone else show us another "sad" shape close to the first one.' Ask the class if the two children have made an 'interesting' picture. Is this because they have chosen, for example:

   a contrasting levels, but focusing on each other
   b the same level, making exactly the same shape back to back or side by side
   c to mirror each other
   d to be in contact with each other, perhaps leaning gently on each other
   e to make the same shape with the top part of their bodies, but with one standing and one kneeling?

   Obviously, there are no right answers, but encourage the children to be aware of some of the possibilities.

2 'Choose a partner. Show each other your sad sequence and decide how you can work together. You must include at least one moment when you have contrasting levels and at least one moment when you are in contact with each other. Practise your new sequence together.'

C Dance

1 'Dance your own angry section, finishing in the space where you have been working with your partner.'

2 'Dance your sad duo.'

3 'Dance your own happy section by yourself.'

D Conclusion

Look at some of the dances.

Obviously, partnerwork could also be introduced in each of the other two sections. This will depend on how long you think the material will continue to hold the interest of the class. The angry section of the dance lends itself particularly well to canon and unison, with one of the pair, A, dancing **1a** and **1b** of the framework followed by the other partner, B, dancing the repeat, finishing next to A so that they can be ready for the sad duo.

Follow my leader, meeting and parting and joining with a partner, work particularly well in the happy section.

If partnerwork is attempted in each section, then the whole dance will probably last for about five or six lessons.

Year 2:
Lesson plans for gymnastics

Pathways (straight / zigzag / curving)

This unit of work is written in four lessons, but will take much longer to teach.

Lesson 1

A Warm-up

1 'Run in and out of each other avoiding contact – stop. Every time I call "Stop", you must stay very still and be in a space.' Repeat this several times.

2 'Be aware of other people – dodge in and out of them and aim for the spaces.' Try again several times.

3 'Run in and out of each other – on command, bounce on the spot. If you feel you are not in a good space, just bounce gently into one.' Repeat several times.

B Floorwork

1 'Stand in a space – on a signal, run in a straight line to another space. What do you do if you meet other people on the way? – either stop until they have passed or, if they stop first, carry on running to your place. Eyes open – be aware of other people.' Repeat this task several times to establish the principle that they must run in an absolutely straight line – no kinks!

2 'Run to three different places, always going in straight lines. Try to make an interesting pattern on the floor with your straight lines'. Choose and show examples of zigzag patterns.

Try again.

3 'Do you always have to travel forwards? You can also travel backwards and sideways. Look over your shoulder when going backwards so there are no collisions.' Choose and show examples, try again.

4 'Can you travel along straight pathways on different body parts? Travel on three straight lines, using different body parts on each line.'

C Apparatus

1 'Explore your own apparatus – over/under/along/through it and so on.'

2 'From whichever side of the apparatus you are on can you approach the apparatus, travel over it, travel away from it, all in a straight line?' Choose and show some examples. Try again.

3 'Can you now use a different line to approach the apparatus, travel over it and away from it?' Show examples and repeat the task.

D Calming-down activity

'Walk with long strides with your body close to the floor.'

Year 2

Lesson **2**

Pathways

Lesson 2

A Warm-up

1 'Can you travel round the room in short, sharp bursts of speed?' Repeat the task several times.

2 'Can you travel in a short straight line, then stop and turn to face in a new direction?' Repeat several times. Now ask the children to move in their own time – short, sharp runs in and out of each other, making angular pathways.

3 'Can you travel round the room making large curved pathways avoiding contact with other people?' Explain to children that they should lead with the shoulder into the curve.

B Floorwork

1 'Travel in large curves again, and this time use your shoulders to lead you into the curve – don't forget you can travel in different directions.'

2 'Can you alter the size of your curved patterns on the floor? You might include a small circle or spin.'

3 'Travel making curving pathways, taking your weight on your hands and feet.' The children will all probably be travelling forwards again, so develop sideways and other directions – choose some examples and let everyone try them out. 'Whichever direction your body is travelling in, you must be tracing a curve on the floor.'

4 'Can you trace a large curvy letter on the floor? For example, s, n, m, c, o, u. Trace it first with your feet, then travel along it on different body parts.' Show some examples. Ask children if they can recognise the letter. Are they changing body parts taking weight along the curves? All try.

C Apparatus

1 'Explore your own apparatus – over/under/along/through it and so on.'

2 'Use your apparatus travelling on hands and feet.'

3 'Can you travel in curved pathways on your apparatus, changing constantly the parts which take your weight?'

D Calming-down activity

'Move slowly round the hall, sometimes taking weight on hands and feet and sometimes sideways rolling.'

Lesson 3

A Warm-up

1 'Travel round the room in short, sharp, fast zigzags avoiding contact with anyone else. Remember to take a large last step before you turn into another direction.'

2 'Trace short zigzag patterns on the floor, travelling on hands and feet.'

3 'Sometimes travel along curved pathways and sometimes short, straight lines.'

B Floorwork

1 'If we travel in short, straight lines it helps to give us speed – which movements would be good to use at the end of a short straight line? (Pause) Jump. Try to run and jump, landing on two feet.'

Remind children to keep their heads up, to swing arms to assist flight, to push from knees, ankles and feet. Practise several times.

2 'Can you jump to land on two feet, but land facing in a different direction?' Let the children experiment and choose examples of 1/4, 1/2, 3/4 and full turns. 'Remember to use your arms to help the turn. Try again. Whichever way you are facing at the completion of your jump, run off in that direction to jump again, so that you make a zigzag pattern.'

3 'Can you trace a large square on the floor and travel along its lines in different ways?'

4 'Can you now trace a pattern on the floor which has both a straight line and a curved line in it, and travel along it on different body parts?' Allow time for children to complete the task and then choose and show some examples.

C Apparatus

1 'Explore your own apparatus – over/under/along/through it and so on.'

2 'Travel on to the apparatus, turn round and travel back to where you started from, using straight lines.'

3 'Travel, using an interesting pathway on the apparatus, sometimes using straight lines, sometimes using curved pathways and sometimes using zigzags.'

D Calming-down activity

'Walk and trot showing good style. Stop on a signal and stand showing a good position.'

Lesson 4

This develops into elementary partner work, with the emphasis on leading and following.

A Warm-up

1 'Practise travelling on hands and feet anywhere in the hall?'

2 'Run/hop/skip/gallop along an interesting pathway anywhere in the hall – don't forget to travel in different directions.'

B Floorwork

1 'Find a partner. A travels along an interesting pathway around the room and B follows exactly the same pathway.' Remind the class that A must not travel too fast and leave B behind; A must make the pattern clear enough for B to follow easily. Change over so that B becomes the leader. Emphasise the importance of the pathway.

2 This time A travels using running, skipping, hopping and galloping, and B follows – the mode of travel is now important. Change over leaders.

3 Now choose any way of travelling. Partner copies and follows – change leaders on a signal.

4 A leads and travels along a floor pattern which is made up of a straight line and a curved line, changing his/her way of travelling for each. B follows. Change over leaders when the pathway is complete. Choose and show examples to highlight changes of level and speed. Let everyone try again.

C Apparatus

1 'Explore your apparatus – over/under/along/through it and so on.'

2 'Working individually, can you find an interesting pathway to travel along on your apparatus? Perform it several times so you will remember it.'

3 A makes the pathway and B follows. Change over.

4 'Can you find an interesting starting position and finishing position?'

'Travel using an interesting pathway.'

D Calming-down activity

'In pairs, one runs around the hall, sometimes quickly, sometimes slowly and partners stay close behind.'

Work unit: Year 3

Aims of unit

1 To introduce the concept of working with a partner.

2 To increase awareness and quality of performance of:

  a Dynamics
  b Weight transference.

Objectives	Lesson 1		Lesson 2		Lesson 3		Lesson 4		Lesson 5		Lesson 6	
	Dance	Gym	Dance	Gym	Dance	Gym	Dance	Gym	Dance	Gym	Dance	Gym
To improve the child's ability to show, use and identify												
Weight transference	☑	✓	✓	✓		☑		✓	✓			✓
Sudden movements ✗	☑	✓	✓	✓	✓		(✓)	✓	(✓)		(✓)	
Legato movements ✗	☑		✓		✓		(✓)		(✓)	✓	(✓)	
Movement on different levels	✓		✓	✓		✓		✓				✓
Jumping actions	✓		✓	☑		✓						✓
Complex step patterns									✓			
To enable the child to show, use and identify some possibilities of working with a partner												
Using canon and unison		✓	☑									
Mirroring a partner's movements ✗						☑		☑	✓	☑		☑
Matching a partner's movements				☑		☑		☑				

Key: ☑ a main emphasis in the lesson   ✓ an emphasis in the lesson

All three aspects of each activity, i.e. composing, performing and appreciating in dance, and planning, performing and evaluating in gymnastics, should be apparent in every lesson.

Assessment

This should relate directly to the overall aims of the unit and the specific objectives for each lesson.

Dances within unit

Lessons 1–2   Cats
♪ *Accompaniment:*   Voice and percussion
  Resources: 'Cat' by Eleanor Farjeon (see page 91)

Lesson 3   Snow
♪ *Accompaniment:*   Voice
  Resources: None required

Lessons 4–6   Funfair Mirrors
Accompaniment: No 8 on the cassette
Resources: None required

Gymnastics within unit

Lessons 1-6   Matching and mirroring

Year 3: Cross-curricular links (Key Stage 2)

Science

- From books find out about the tracks made by birds and animals in the snow. Try to identify any tracks that may be found in the local environment.
- Investigate the needs of various animals and compare these with human needs. Create a suitable habitat in the classroom for mini-beasts. Learn how to care for pets.
- Investigate the differences between images produced in curved and flat mirrors. Make and use a kaleidoscope.

Mathematics

- Research class members' pets. Design and produce a data collection sheet and present results graphically.

Cats

Funfair mirrors

Technology

- Design and make a funfair ride.

English

- Describe a snowy day in a letter to a friend who has never seen snow. Talk about how snow looks and feels and the sort of activities such as sledging and snowball fights that take place in the snow.
- Find words that describe the ways in which different animals move.
- Write a description of an exciting ride.

Art

- Look at different patterns that snowflakes make. Paint different snowflake patterns in white paint on black paper.
- Look at pictures of winter scenes painted by such artists as Brueghel, Pissaro, Utrillo and discuss the ways in which they have treated the same theme.
- Do the same with pictures showing animals by artists such as Gaugin, Rousseau and Chagall.
- Draw reflections that appear in mirrors, puddles and spoons.
- Make a life-sized model of a cat from card by cutting, scoring, folding and gluing.

History

- Find out about the worst winters in Great Britain and their effects on ordinary people. Talk to grandparents about the winter of 1947.

Snow

Music

- Sing rounds in two parts (using canon). Echo musical phases using words, rhythms, body parts and melodies.
- Select instruments and make short pieces to show the different moods of snow.

Year 3: Lesson plans for dance

Cats

Before the lesson the children should have had the opportunity to observe cats, finding words to describe their actions (e.g. pounce, spit, arch) and how they move (e.g. very smoothly, as they stretch and very suddenly, when they pounce). They should also be familiar with the poem 'Cat' by Eleanor Farjeon.

CAT

Cat!
Scat!
Atter her, atter her,
Sleeky flatterer
Spitfire chatterer,
Scatter her, scatter her
Off her mat!
Wuff!
Wuff!
Treat her rough!
Git her, git her,
Whiskery spitter!
Catch her, catch her,
green-eyed scratcher!
Slathery
Slithery
Hisser,
Don't miss her!
Run till you're dithery,
Hithery
thithery
Pfitts! pfitts!
How she spits!
Spitch! Spatch!
Can't she scratch!
Scritching the bark
Of the sycamore-tree
She's reached her ark
and's hissing at me
Pfitts! pfitts!
Wuff! wuff!
Scat,
Cat!
That's
That!

Dance framework

1 'Sleeky flattery' section – individual smooth, stretching, arching movements linked by rolls.

2 'Pfitts, pfitts/How she spits' section – partner dance to include sharp, sudden movements with leaps and rolls and the use of canon and unison.

Year 3

Lesson 1

Cats

Lesson 1

A Introduction

1 'Run into a space and freeze.'

2 'Run into a space and freeze close to the floor and explode into a jump, filling as much space as possible.' Repeat several times.

B Movement exploration and development

1 'On hands and knees, see if you can arch your back up to the ceiling like a cat does. Don't forget to drop your head. Now see if you can lift your head and curve your back the other way so that your middles are pulled towards the floor.'

'Can you move smoothly from one shape to the other?'

2 'Lie on your side with your arms above your head and your legs straight. Arch backwards like a banana. Now see if you can curve forwards.'

3 'Can you stretch into curved shapes while you are kneeling?' Emphasise:

a stretching sideways as well as forwards and backwards

b smooth, continuous movement so that one stretch goes into another like yawning.

Encourage twisting and rolling from one movement to another. Suggest changes of level. Use 'sleeky flatterer' from the poem, repeated several times as the vocal accompaniment, said either by you or by the children.

4 'Show me your fingers as if they were claws.'

5 'Show me how quickly you can shoot out your fingers into the space around you. Do you use one hand or two, or one after the other; in the same or different directions? Use different levels.' Emphasise use of the whole body to make sudden movements.

6 'Can you show me two sharp movements as I say "Pfitts, pfitts"? Now roll sideways smoothly, transferring your weight on to your knees before you make another sharp movement – as I say "How she spits!", making your sharp movement on the word "spits".'

'Let's now try that again, but this time transfer your weight on to your feet after the roll.'

7 'Run and jump into the air, shooting your arms and legs into the space around you, as I say "How she spits!". Make sure that you jump when I say "spits". As you land from your jump, freeze with your fingers stretched out like a cat's claws.'

C Dance

1 'Practise the smooth, stretching curving, movements using "sleeky flatterer" as the accompaniment. (The words "sleeky flatterer" should be said at least three times.)

Practise the spitting phrase, i.e.

"Pfitts, pfitts" (two sharp movements)

"How she spits" (roll, transfer weight, sharp movement).

Repeat this

"How she spits!" (run, leap and land)'

D Conclusion

'Lie on the floor and imagine the sound of a cat purring. Gently stand up and walk to the door.'

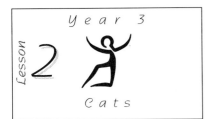

Year 3

Lesson 2

Cats

Lesson 2

A Introduction

1 'Practise the smooth "sleeky flatterer" section of your dance.'

2 'Practise the sharp movements.'

3 'Practise the whole dance learned so far.
   a 'Smooth, stretching, arching and curving movements to the words "sleeky flatterer", which should be repeated three times.'
   b 'The spitting phrase of two sharp movements, roll, transference of weight and another sharp movement to "Pfitts, pfitts/How she spits!". Repeat this finishing on your feet ready to run and jump into the air for the final phrase of "How she spits!". Finish with your hands stretched out like claws.'

C Movement exploration and development

1 'Find a partner. Using the material you have made for the second section of the dance, let's make it into a partner dance. You must use canon and unison. Make your accompaniment from the words "Pfitts, pfitts/How she spits!", but you can decide how many times to repeat them.'

If you feel your class needs more help with this task, then you might decide to use the following suggested outline:

'Pfitts! pfitts! *How she spits!'*	A dances (2 sharp movements, roll, transfer weight, sharp movement).
'Pfitts! pfitts! *How she spits!'*	B dances own version of the phrase.
'How she spits! *How she spits!* *How she spits!'*	A runs, leaps and lands. B runs, leaps and lands. A and B run, leap and land together.

C Dance

'Dance the "sleeky flatterer" section alone, but near your partner, then you dance the "Pfitts, pfitts/How she spits!" section with your partner.'

D Conclusion

Look at the dances and comment on them.

Snow

Dance framework

1 'Whoosh' – travel with turns using high and low levels.

2 'Splot' – finish in a two-dimensional shape facing a partner.

3 'Slurp' – mirroring each other's movements as they slide down to the floor together.

Lesson 3

A Introduction

1 'Run anywhere in the room and freeze your movement when I hit the tambourine.' Repeat several times.

2 'Do the same and this time sink down slowly on to the ground after your freeze.' Repeat.

B Movement exploration and development

Discuss the different ways in which snow falls – often it falls softly and gently, but sometimes during snow storms the snow swirls and is driven against windows where it sticks before it eventually melts.

1 'Let's imagine that there is a snow storm. Show me how you can swirl from one place to another.' Encourage travelling using different levels with turns and jumps. Encourage the use of different body parts to lead the movement, e.g. shoulders, heads, elbows, fingers.

2 'If you meet a flat surface, such as a window or a wall, show me how you would stop.' Encourage a sudden two-dimensional stop.

3 'Let's practise swirling and stopping.' Repeat several times.

4 'Show me now how you might slide down the window slowly and smoothly, finishing in a flat position on the floor because the snow has melted to form a puddle.'

5 'Find a partner and go into a space and face each other. Imagine that there is a wall of glass between you. See if you can slide down the wall at the same time as each other. Try to mirror your partner's movements. One of you lead the movement first and then change over.'

C Dance

'Dance your swirling section one after the other, finishing in your flat shape against the wall. Melt and slide down the wall together to finish in a wide, flat shape.'

The accompaniment for the dance could be words said by the children, e.g. 'whoosh' as they swirl, 'splat' as they hit the wall and 'slurp' as they slide down and melt. When the words are said by the children as they dance, the dynamic qualities of their movement improve considerably.

D Conclusion

Look at some of the dances and comment upon them.

Funfair mirrors

Dance framework

1 **a** Mirroring partner's movements, grow slowly and collapse suddenly. Repeat.

   b Grow in stages and jump backwards away from partners.

2 **a** Bounces, hops and jumps on the spot for 16 beats.

   b Skips, jumps, hops and bounces for 16 beats travelling away from and towards partners, still mirroring each other's movements.

3 A leaps sideways followed by B.

4 Individual sequence of running, leaping, spinning and turning anywhere in the room.

Year 3

Lesson

4

Funfair mirrors

Lesson 4

A Introduction

Jumping, skipping, travelling and turning anywhere in the room. Use some lively music.

B Movement exploration and development

1 'Face me and mirror my movements.' The teacher gallops sideways and then to the left and then skips forwards and backwards.

2 'Now see if you can mirror my movements on the spot.' The teacher 'grows' into different shapes and then shrinks down suddenly to the ground. Sometimes the growing is continuous and involves the whole body moving at the same time; sometimes specific parts of the body lead the movement and sometimes the body moves and stops before continuing to grow again.

3 'Find a partner and go into a space. Imagine that you are at a fair and have gone into a hall of mirrors. With your partner, grow and shrink into different shapes, as if you are looking into a mirror. Take it in turns to lead the movement. Grow into your shapes slowly and shrink down quickly. Choose two of your favourite ways of doing this and practise them. Remember to mirror your partner's movements.'

4 'Show me now how you can grow in stages. Take it in turns to lead the movement.'

5 'Let's put those two ideas together, i.e. grow and shrink twice, then grow in stages and freeze.'

6 'After you freeze, see if you can jump away from each other. Remember you are still looking in the mirror.'

C Dance

'Practise the dance – grow and shrink and repeat; grow in stages and jump away from each other. You then break away from your partner, skipping, turning and jumping, enjoying your freedom.'

D Conclusion

Look at some of the dances and comment on them.

Lesson 5

A Introduction

Repeat as Lesson 4

B Movement exploration and development

1 'Practise the mirroring sequence you made last lesson.'

2 'Using hops and bounces, make up a sequence on the spot which lasts for eight counts. Include hopping and bouncing from side to side and forwards and backwards.'

3 'Show your sequence to your partner and then mirror it. Try both sequences. Put both sequences together so that the whole sequence lasts for 16 counts.'

C Dance

Practise Nos 1 and 2a of the framework.

D Conclusion

Any relaxation exercise.

Lesson 6

A Introduction

Recap the dance learned last time.

B Movement exploration and development

1 Explain the dance. 'Discover your image in the mirror as you shrink and grow, then try to trick the image with the hopping and bouncing sequence. You are now going to make a sequence with your partner still using hops, bounces and also skips to travel away from each other and then back towards each other.'

2 'You have not been able to get rid of each other, so you try leaping sideways. You suddenly find that you have managed to lose your reflection. Let's practise that: A leaps sideways and then B leaps sideways. You are now free.'

3 'Run and leap and spin and roll, enjoying your freedom.'

C Dance

Practise the whole dance as in the framework.

D Conclusion

Look at the dances and discuss them.

Year 3: Lesson plans for gymnastics

Matching and mirroring

Lesson 1

A Warm-up

1 'Run in and out of each other without making contact. Stop.' Repeat several times.

2 'See how quickly you can sit down/stand up/lie down/walk in and out of each other/sit.' Make this into a game-like activity.

B Floorwork

1 'Sit down – travel on your bottom in different ways.' Show some examples. Let everyone try the different ideas.

2 'Lie down on your front or back or side-travel round the room in any way possible.' Show examples of different ideas and let everyone try them.

3 'Show all the different ways you can travel round the room, taking weight on different parts in different ways.' Choose some examples of unusual ways of travelling and let everyone try them.

4 'Find a partner; stand one behind the other – the front one must be aware of their partner and not run too fast so your partner can keep up. Follow my leader in and out of all the other pairs, using all the room and avoiding contact. Change over on command.'

5 'Try this now with the leader travelling in different ways. Change the way of travelling frequently. Change over on command.'

C Apparatus

1 'Explore the apparatus travelling over/under/along/through it and so on.'

2 'By yourself, follow a pathway going over/under/along/through your apparatus travelling in different ways. Make up a short pathway so you can repeat it.'

3 'Get into pairs. A leads on his/her pathway as B follows, then B leads and A follows.'

D Calming-down activity

Find various balances on one body part.'

Lesson 2

A Warm-up

1 'Travel round the room in different ways – on command stop in a position close to the floor.'

2 'Run in and out of each other – on command stop in a high position. Travel round the room as far away from the floor as possible.'

3 'Travel round the room, sometimes far away from the floor, sometimes close to it.'

B Floorwork

1 'With a partner, follow my leader; stand side by side with your partner. Can you find a way of travelling which you can do together, side by side?' Allow time for experimentation, then show examples of sideways rolling, sliding, running and jumping, etc.

Are they doing exactly the same movements as each other – if they are walking or running, are they both moving at the same time? Practise again to get the movements precise. If a travelling movement is to be matching, partners must move the same part of the body at the same time as each other.

2 'Can you travel side by side close to the ground, and then far away from the ground, matching exactly?' Give time for experimentation and then choose and show some examples.

3 Look at ideas of jumping and ask the children to do a matching jump with their partners.

C Apparatus

'Explore your own apparatus and find where you can:

a do a matching jump together to the ground

b travel across the apparatus or from it showing matching movement.'

Matching jump with a partner.

D Calming-down activity

Travel round the hall in pairs, one copying accurately the movements of the other.'

Lesson 3

A Warm-up

1 Trot in and out of each other; when you see a good space, run and jump into it.' Comment and remind the children about keeping heads up and using arms to get lift into the air.

2 'Run and jump into spaces showing different shaped jumps. Choose and show examples of star, stretched, curled and twisted shapes in the air.

B Floorwork

1 'Run around the room; when you come to a good space, jump into it, sink down and roll away sideways.' Teach the safety points of bending knees to land and sink down carefully into the sideways roll. Practise the sideways roll.

2 'Can you and your partner perform the same two movements – a jump and a sideways roll exactly together?

3 'Can you and your partner now find a balanced position you can move into after the sideways roll? Practise your sequence – jump, sideways roll and balance, matching your partner exactly. Remember to hold your balance for three seconds. Keep your bodies tight and strong to hold your balance.'

B Apparatus

1 Explore your apparatus individually, over/under/along/through it and so on.'

2 'Find places on your apparatus where you can jump down to land on your feet and roll away. Don't forget the different shapes you can make in the air. Remember to land on two feet and, in a tucked jump, you must keep your head up and bring your knees up to your chest.'

3 'With a partner, travel towards your apparatus, use your apparatus and travel away from it with a jump and roll away. Your movements must match, but remember they can be on different levels.'

D Calming-down activity

'Travel round the hall showing extreme positions of stretched or curled positions.'

Lesson 4

A Warm-up

1 'Run in and out of each other avoiding contact – stop in a balanced position.' Repeat this several times.

2 'Shoot into a different balance position every time I clap my hands. Remember you can balance on large body parts and small ones. Repeat. Try to produce a different balance each time.' Remind children to make their bodies feel tight and stretched.

B Floorwork

1 'With a partner, work out some ideas for balances, with some close to the floor and some far away from it.'

2 'Decide, with your partner, on two favourite balances, and join them together, matching with your partner.'

3 Give time to experiment and work out the sequence – they should still be performing side by side or one behind the other.

4 'Now add run, jump and sink down into a roll before you perform your two balances.' Give the children time to experiment and then show some examples of sequences.

C Apparatus

1 'Individually explore your apparatus – over/under/along/through it and so on.'

2 'Find places on your apparatus where you can hold a balanced position – move on and balance on another part of the apparatus.'

3 'With a partner, find places on the apparatus where you can perform matching balances – remember you don't have to be on the same part of the apparatus or even on the same level.'

4 'Join two matching balances together and leave the apparatus with a matching jump, sink down and roll away.' Give children time to experiment. Show examples of sequences.

D Calming-down activity

'Travel on hands and feet covering the whole floor space of the hall.'

Year 3

Lesson 5

Matching and mirroring

Lesson 5

A Warm-up

1 'Travel round the hall taking weight from your hands and back to your feet.'

2 'Take weight from your feet to your hands to your feet again on the spot.'

3 'In pairs – one lying on the floor – the other should travel over, taking weight on their hands at some point.'

B Floorwork

1 'Face each other as if looking in a mirror, with hands touching your partner's palms. One partner slowly moves a hand in a circular polishing movement, the other mirrors the movement.'

2 'Try moving both hands to polish the mirror. Move hands towards and away from the mirror.' From this exercise it can be shown that, to mirror movements, the opposite hand, arm, leg, etc, moves – just like looking at a reflection in a mirror.

3 'Face your partner – one of you slowly stretches and curls, while the other mirrors the actions.' Change over the prime mover.

4 'Start about 5 metres away from your partner – you should be facing. Make up a short mirror sequence travelling towards the mirror and away, sideways along the face of the mirror and up and down.'

C Apparatus

1 'Explore your own apparatus – under/over/along/through it and so on.'

2 'Find different ways of getting on to the apparatus and off it.'

3 'In pairs, approach the apparatus from opposite sides and travel on to the apparatus, mirroring your partner's movements, and travel back off the apparatus.'

D Calming-down activity

'Move using hands and feet only.'

Year 3

Lesson 6

Matching and mirroring

Lesson 6

A Warm-up

1 'Move freely, sometimes slowly, sometimes quickly, avoiding contact with other people.'

2 'Trot three paces and jump to land in different balanced positions – move in your own time.'

3 'With a partner, walk side by side mirroring each other's actions. (Remember to use opposite arms and legs.) Try trotting and then running.'

B Floorwork

1 'Make a sequence of run, jump, sink down and roll away – mirroring your partner's actions.'

2 'Make up a sequence mirroring each other, using run, jump, roll and balance, plus a travelling movement.' Remind children about using opposite arm and leg. Allow plenty of time for experimentation and choose examples to illustrate different pathways and speeds.

C Apparatus

1 'As individuals, explore the apparatus under/over/along/through it.'

2 'Find places on the apparatus where you can mirror a balance with your partner. Remember you need not be on the same part of the apparatus or the same level.' Show some examples and try again.

3 'Mirroring your partner's movements, travel on to the apparatus; move into a balance and then move over or along the apparatus and off.' Allow time for experimentation and then look at demonstrations of sequences. Are they mirroring? Are they at different levels? Are they travelling at different speeds and in different directions? If not, practise again, before looking at all the sequences.

D Calming-down activity

'Run and jump to touch toes with hands in various ways.'

Work unit: Year 4

Aims of unit

1 To introduce the concept of symmetric and asymmetric movement
2 To improve the dynamic range of the class.

Objectives	Lesson 1		Lesson 2		Lesson 3		Lesson 4		Lesson 5		Lesson 6	
	Dance	Gym	Dance	Gym	Dance	Gym	Dance	Gym	Dance	Gym	Dance	Gym
To enable the child to show, use and identify												
Symmetric movements	☑	☑	✓	☑	✓	☑	☑			✓	✓	✓
Asymmetric movements	☑		☑		✓		✓	☑		✓	✓	✓
To improve the performance, use and knowledge of:												
Body shape in stillness and motion	✓	✓	☑	✓	☑	✓	☑	✓	✓		✓	✓
Weight transference	☑	☑	☑	✓	✓	✓	✓	✓	✓	☑	✓	✓
Movement on different levels	✓	✓		✓		✓		✓		✓	✓	✓
Legato movements	✓		✓		✓		✓		✓		✓	
Staccato movements			✓		✓		✓				✓	
Strong movements		✓	☑	✓	☑		☑	✓	✓		✓	✓
Canon and unison in pairs			✓		✓		✓				✓	
Canon and unison in fours									☑		✓	

Key: ☑ a main emphasis in the lesson   ✓ an emphasis in the lesson

All three aspects of each activity, i.e. composing, performing and appreciating
in dance, and planning, performing and evaluating in gymnastics, should be
apparent in every lesson.

Assessment

This should relate directly to the overall aims of the unit and the specific
objectives for each lesson.

Dances within unit

Lessons 1–6 Oriental adventure
♪ *Accompaniment:* No 9 on the cassette
Resources: Fans, illustrations of martial arts,
including karate and sumo
wrestling

Gymnastics within unit

Lessons 1–6 Symmetry and asymmetry

Year 4: Cross-curricular links (Key Stage 2)

Oriental adventure

Music

- Use the pentatonic scale to produce a short piece with an oriental flavour.

Mathematics

- Study shapes and identify some lines of symmetry and asymmetry
- Investigate which letters and numbers have reflective/rotational lines of symmetry.
- Turn shapes using tracing paper.

Art

- Study and use origami techniques.
- Look at the different ways in which the flower motif is used in different cultures, including those of Japan and China. Develop a drawing of a flower into a motif for appliqué and embroidery.

Technology

- Design and make a fan.

History

- Look at Japanese and/or Chinese calligraphy in terms of pattern and meaning. Make and draw/paint sentences based on the words studied.

English

- Describe the mood inspired by a Japanese watercolour.
- Look at examples of haiku poems. Write poems using this form, i.e. three lines containing a total of 17 syllables. The first line has five syllables, the second has seven and the third has five.

Movement emphasis — symmetry and asymmetry

Year 4:
Lesson plans for dance _____

Oriental adventure

Dance framework

1 Solo fan section based on symmetric and asymmetric opening and closing movements linked by spinning and turning movements on different levels.

2 Karate section in pairs. As dance their phrase of run, jump, roll and freeze. Bs dance their phrase of run, jump, roll and freeze. Repeat with Bs finishing next to their partners.

3 Partner sumo section based on slow-motion wrestling movements.

4 Each pair travels to meet another pair to dance their group fan dance based on the movement of the spokes of a fan.

Year 4

Lesson 1

Oriental adventure

Lesson 1

A Introduction

1 'Stretch as high as possible and curl up as small as possible.' Repeat several times.

2 'Stretch as high as possible, then spread both arms out to the side and spin down into a curled shape again.'

3 'Run smoothly into a space, stretch up tall, spread your arms out and spin gently down.' Repeat several times.

B Movement exploration and development

Using a fan as a stimulus, show how it opens and closes. Does it open symmetrically or asymmetrically? Is it in an asymmetric or symmetric shape when it is closed?

'What happens if one side of the fan is opened first, followed by the other side? The opening is asymmetric, but the final position is symmetric.'

1 'Let's play with some of these ideas of opening and closing, using the movements of the fan to help us. Starting in a tall position, show me how you can spread your arms to finish in an open fan shape and close back in again to hold your tall shape.' Emphasise that one arm may open out first, followed by the other and similarly they may close one after the other. Encourage the children to open into the forwards and backwards dimension as well as the sideways one. Ensure that the movements are performed as smoothly as possible.

Show some examples, asking the children to pick out some symmetric shapes and some asymmetric ones.

2 'Lie on the floor in a long thin shape as if the fan were closed. Show me now how you can spread your arms and your legs to open symmetrically. Let's try it now, opening asymmetrically.'

3 'Show me how you can spread into your fan shape when supporting your weight on different parts of the body. Perhaps you could try sitting or kneeling. Perhaps you could make your fan shape by using an arm and a leg at the same time.' Remind children of the two-dimensional movement of the fan as it is opened and closed.

C Dance

'Choose at least four opening and closing movements and see if you can join them together using gentle spins and rolls. You should include the use of:

a both symmetric and asymmetric opening and closing movements

b different levels

c weight supported on different body parts.'

D Conclusion

'Show your phrase to a partner who will check that you have included the use of both symmetric and asymmetric movements as you move into your fan shapes.'

Year 4

Lesson 2

Oriental adventure

Lesson 2

A Introduction

'Practise the dance you made in the last lesson.'

B Movement exploration and development

1 'You remember how we talked in the classroom about the martial arts of the orient. Show me now a still position, like a photograph, of someone doing karate.' Emphasise the strength and angularity of the movement. Point out that the positions tend to be asymmetric.

2 'Show me a small jump before you freeze in your "karate" shape. Now make that a huge jump.'

'Make sure you have plenty of space around you and see if you can kick and punch into the air before landing.'

'Let's add a short run as a preparation for the jump and freeze.'

3 'Show one of your karate "photographs" again. See how you can gently lower yourself to the ground from the photograph. When you reach the ground, roll gently, then freeze into another karate photograph.' Practise several times.

'Perhaps you could roll and jump up on to your feet again before you freeze, or you may freeze while you are on your knees.'

4 'Let's practise jumping high and finishing low, so that you can go straight into your roll.'

C Dance

'Dance the fan section, followed by run, jump, roll and freeze. Repeat the run, jump, roll and freeze phrase three more times.'

D Conclusion

Any relaxation exercise.

Lesson 3

A Introduction

1 'Run anywhere in the room and when I hit the tambourine, freeze in a karate shape.' Emphasise the angularity and asymmetric nature of the shape. Practise several times.

2 'Run and jump, punching and kicking your arms and legs in the air as you jump to finish in a karate photograph.'

3 'Recap the whole of your karate phrase, i.e. run, jump, roll and freeze.' Repeat several times.

B Movement exploration and development

1 'Find a partner. Name yourselves A and B. Find a space away from your partner. All As dance your karate phrase. Now all Bs dance your karate phrase. All As dance your karate phrase again. All Bs dance yours, but this time you must finish within 2 metres of your partner.' Practise this again.

2 'Look at the combined shape you are making with your partner. Will you both finish on the same level? Is it symmetric or asymmetric? Are you in contact with each other? Decide how you want your combined photograph to be.'

C Dance

With a partner, dance Nos 1 and 2 of the framework, i.e. the fan section followed by the karate section. Practise several times.

D Conclusion

Any relaxation exercise.

Lesson 4

A Introduction

Any stretching exercises.

B Movement exploration and development

1 'Let's look at some photographs of sumo wrestlers.' Show photographs of wrestlers in symmetric and asymmetric poses. Ask the children to differentiate between the two.

2 'Let's try copying some of these photographs. Show me first of all a symmetric pose. Remember how the wrestler bends his knees and has his feet quite wide apart.

'Lean forward and place both hands on your knees. Now try lifting one leg and making an asymmetric shape. Which of the two positions feels safer? Why is this?' Establish that a wide base and a low centre of gravity are much more stable than a high centre of gravity and a narrow base. Symmetric shapes also look, and usually are, stronger and more powerful than asymmetric ones.

You can show this by standing in a symmetric shape and inviting one of the class to try and push you over, then show how much easier it is to be pushed over from an asymmetric shape.

3 'Find the partner with whom you were working last week. Face each other and place your hands on each other's shoulders. In slow motion, push each other sideways, first to one side and then to the other.' A then pushes B slowly to the floor.

'Try the same idea with B pushing A to the floor.'

'Perhaps you could turn your partners as you push them down. Perhaps you could spin them around when they are on the floor.'

4 'You remember that the wrestlers bow to each other before their fight begins. Use this idea at the beginning of your wrestling sequence. Some of the wrestlers also throw salt over their shoulders for good luck at the beginning of their fight. You might like to use this idea as well.'

'Describe how you are going to finish your sequence. Will one person win or will it be a draw? Show me your finishing positions.' Practise the whole sequence.

C Dance

1 Recap the karate sequence.

2 Dance the karate sequence followed by the sumo sequence.

D Conclusion

Any calming-down activity.

Sumo wrestling dance sequence.

Year 4

Lesson 5

Oriental adventure

Lesson 5

A Introduction

Repeat as for Lesson 1.

B Movement exploration and development

1 'Look at the fans again and especially the wooden spokes. Notice how they are joined at the bottom and how they radiate out, as the fan is opened, and overlap one behind the other, as the fan is closed. Find the partner you worked with last time, then join another pair. In your group of four, stand one behind the other and experiment with the idea of making a fan shape involving everyone in the group. Make your arms look like the spokes of the fan as they radiate out. Now bring your arms back as if the fan is being closed. You could try the same idea using your legs.' Encourage the idea of canon and unison.

'Listen to the music and decide how many times you want to repeat your sequence. Finish as if the fan has been opened.' Practise.

'Show me your group's starting position. Look at the space where you are now. This is the space to which you will return for this part of the dance.'

2 'With your partner from last week, go and stand where you finished at the end of the sumo section. With very small steps, run into your starting position for the group fan dance.'

C Dance

Recap the sumo section. Dance the sumo section followed by the group fan dance, i.e. sections 3 and 4 of the framework.

D Conclusion

Look at and discuss the group fan dances.

Year 4

Lesson

6

Oriental adventure

Lesson 6

Practise all four sections of the dance and perform them for each other.

Year 4:
Lesson plans for gymnastics _____

Symmetry and asymmetry

Lesson 1

A Warm-up

1 Ask the children to stand up, sit down, kneel down, lie down, etc. in different orders. Do the children respond quickly to the instructions? Make a game of it.

2 'Run in and out of each other – stop like statues.' Encourage different positions.

B Floorwork

1 'Stretch high – as high as possible. Curl up low, making your body as tight as possible – head in, elbows in, etc.' Repeat several times, reminding them about tension in the stretch.

2 'What shape is the stretched movement – even or uneven?' Establish that it is symmetrical. 'Are there any other symmetrical shapes you can make? Do you always have to do a shape standing on your feet? Do you always have to do a stretched shape?' Let the children try out the ideas and then show examples of different ideas.

3 'Is it possible to travel along the ground in a symmetrical shape?' You could demonstrate examples of sliding, bounces on two feet, jumps from two feet to two feet.

4 'Put your hands on the floor, arms straight, head up, push your bottom up into the air – remember to use strong arms.'

5 'Using the same idea of strong arms with hands on the floor, head up, can you travel in a bouncing way and still be symmetrical? Let's try out some ideas.'

C Apparatus

1 'Explore the apparatus – over/under/around/through it.'

2 'Travel round the hall in a symmetrical way and then use the apparatus when you come to a clear piece.'

3 'Travel around the hall in a symmetrical way, and use the apparatus in a symmetrical way when it is clear.'

D Calming-down activity

'Run and jump to show different shapes in the air.'

Lesson 2

A Warm-up

1 Stand up/sit down, lie down/kneel, etc. to command – repeat several times but in different orders.

2 'Can you run anywhere – sit – travel around the room in a sitting position – stand – travel around the room on your feet, etc. going through all the different positions?'

3 'In pairs, A makes a shape on hands and feet. B goes under. Now change over.'

B Floorwork

1 Question the children about symmetrical shapes to remind them of the theme.

2 'Can you travel showing me the different symmetrical shapes you can find to move in?' Show examples of these ideas and all try them out.

3 'Is it possible to travel in a symmetrical way with your legs together?' Use demonstrations to show ideas like bunny hops, forward rolls, jumps, slides and backwards rolls.

4 'Is it possible to travel in a symmetrical way with your legs apart?' Show examples of ideas, e.g. rolls to straddle, cartwheels, star jumps, bunny hops, slides or walks. Let children try out the ideas and then select one and teach it.

5 'Hands on floor, head up, strong arms, push bottom up into the air as high as possible.'

6 'Can you travel round the hall with legs together or apart in a symmetrical way, using bouncing?'

C Apparatus

1 'Explore the apparatus – over/under/round/through it.'

2 'Travel round the hall in a symmetrical way with your legs apart and then use the apparatus when you come to a clear piece.'

3 'Travel round the hall in a symmetrical way with your legs together and then use the apparatus when you come to a clear piece.'

4 'On your own piece of apparatus, use it in a symmetrical way showing legs together or legs apart. Make the movements follow each other smoothly.'

D Calming-down activity

'Move around the hall frequently taking weight on hands in a variety of ways.'

Year 4

Lesson **3**

Symmetry and asymmetry

Lesson 3

A Warm-up

'Move lightly over the floor and, on a signal, jump and make a symmetrical shape in the air – land and continue.' Look for both sides of the body being matched in the jump; the shape could be a star, straight or tucked jump, but to be symmetrical the children must take off from two feet. Remind them not to forget the give of the body on landing.

B Floorwork

1 'Show me all the different ways you can make a symmetrical shape on the floor. Remember you can be on different levels and you can have legs apart or together.'

2 'Move around the hall in a symmetrical way, changing levels.' Choose examples to show good change of levels. Let the children try again.

3 'Now use at least two ways of travelling symmetrically.' Choose and show an example. Ask questions to establish if the task is being answered fully.

C Apparatus

1 'Explore your own apparatus – under/over/around/through it.'

2 'Move over the apparatus in a symmetrical way.' Choose examples to show precise symmetrical movement, the quality of movement, tension in the body, straight legs, pointed toes, etc.

3 'Move between the apparatus with both sides of the body doing the same actions at the same time; travel on to a clear piece of apparatus, hold a symmetrical balance, and move on.' Check that hands and feet are working together and that the children hold the stillness in the balances.

D Calming-down activity

Follow my leader in pairs, frequently changing the leader.

Year 4

Lesson **4**

Symmetry and asymmetry

Lesson 4

A Warm-up

1 'Run forwards/backwards/sideways.' Remind the children about looking over their shoulder when running backwards.

2 'Run in and out of each other, jump and continue.' Repeat this several times.

3 'Run in and out of each other and jump to turn in the air.' Repeat several times. Question/answer about the turning jumps, plus demonstrations, will establish that turning jumps are generally uneven or asymmetrical.

B Floorwork

1 'Stretch up into a star shape, then lean to one side, take one foot off the ground and stretch it out to the side.' Establish that they are now in an asymmetric shape.

2 'Can you find any other asymmetric or uneven shapes you can hold in a balance? Remember you can be on different levels.' Choose and show some examples. Let everyone try them.

Here the children should discover that they rarely have their legs together if the body is making an asymmetric shape, because in the majority of cases the legs work independently or are in different positions. If the legs are together or in the same shape, the arms must be different from each other, or vice versa to make the shape asymmetric.

3 'Can you move from one asymmetrical shape into another one?' Emphasise the stillness of the shape and moving smoothly into the next shape.

4 'Take your weight on your hands and kick one leg up into the air. Remember to make your arms strong and to keep your head up.

'Kick one leg up in the air and change it to come down.'

5 'Can you find ways of rolling asymmetrically?' They could roll sideways or over one shoulder. 'Try starting and finishing in a standing position.'

C Apparatus

1 'Explore your own apparatus.'

2 'Can you find different ways to balance on/under/along apparatus in a symmetric shape?'

3 'Can you travel between the apparatus in a symmetrical way, then use a clear piece of apparatus to hold an asymmetric shape and move on?'

D Calming-down activity

'Move around the hall alternating between normal speed and slow motion.'

Lesson 5

A Warm-up

1 'Run in and out of each other, jump into a space and continue.'

2 'Run in and out of each other, jump into a space showing symmetric and asymmetric jumps – move on and continue.'

3 'Stand/lie down/sit/kneel, then in each position travel in an asymmetric way, e.g. lying on your back, look over your shoulder and walk legs to push yourself around on the floor. Try moving asymmetrically on different parts of the body.'

B Floorwork

1 'Can you find your own way of moving asymmetrically around the hall?' Show some examples and let the children try out the different ideas.

2 'Join together two symmetric balances with an asymmetric travelling action.' Look for stillness in balances and smoothness of transitions.

3 'Can you join together two asymmetric balances with a symmetric travelling action?'

C Apparatus

1 'Explore your apparatus by going over/under/along/through it.'

2 'Can you arrive on your apparatus symmetrically and leave it asymmetrically?'

3 Can you start away from your apparatus, travel towards it, use it, and travel away again, showing both symmetry and asymmetry?' Remind children about change of direction and moving smoothly from one movement to the next.

D Calming-down activity

'Travel round the hall tracing curved patterns on the front.'

Lesson 6

A Warm-up

1 'Run and stop in a shape showing symmetry or asymmetry.' Repeat this several times.

2 'Travel in and out of each other in different ways on different levels – keep changing the way you are travelling.'

Year 4
Lesson 5
Symmetry and asymmetry

Year 4
Lesson 6
Symmetry and asymmetry

3 'In pairs – one person leads, the other follows – travel in different ways. Change over leader.'

B Floorwork

1 'Link together travel/jump/roll in any order showing symmetry and asymmetry.' Let the children have time to complete the task, then choose and show an example. Ask the class:

a Is the child doing everything he/she should be doing?

b Is he/she showing symmetry/asymmetry?

c Is he/she showing different levels?

Give the children another quick turn to make sure they are all doing it correctly.

2 'Having successfully joined together the three movements, now add a balanced position and a movement taking weight on hands to the rest of the sequence.'

3 Let the children work for a few minutes to complete the task – show another example and repeat the above questions. Then ask the children to perform their sequences at the same time and hold their finishing positions until everyone has finished.

C Apparatus

1 'Explore your own apparatus – over/under/around/through it.'

2 'In any order, can you make up a sequence consisting of jump/roll/travel and take weight on hands on your own piece of apparatus, then travel to another piece and hold a balance to finish?

'Remember to show symmetry/asymmetry, different levels, smooth moving from one movement to the next.'

3 Show some individual sequences.

4 Finally, ask the children all to begin at the same time, perform their sequences and hold the finishing position until everyone has finished.

D Calming-down activity.

'Leap as high as possible into the air and turn before landing.'

Work unit: Year 5

Aims of unit

1 To explore some of the compositional possibilities of working in small groups.
2 To increase awareness of curving and linear floor pathways.
3 To develop the concept of enriching movements through variation.

Objectives	Lesson 1		Lesson 2		Lesson 3		Lesson 4		Lesson 5		Lesson 6	
	Dance	Gym	Dance	Gym	Dance	Gym	Dance	Gym	Dance	Gym	Dance	Gym
To enable the child to show, use and identify												
a Different ways of working in a small group to include												
Meeting, parting and avoiding			[✓]		[✓]				[✓]	✓	✓	✓
Canon and unison	[✓]		[✓]		[✓]		[✓]			✓	✓	✓
Copying							[✓]			✓	✓	✓
Making group shapes and formations							[✓]		[✓]		✓	[✓]
b Enriching movement by varying speed, size and level	[✓]		✓	✓	✓	✓		✓	✓			
To improve the child's ability to show, use and identify												
The use of linear and curving pathways	[✓]		✓		[✓]	✓	[✓]			✓	✓	✓
Curved and straight body shapes		[✓]		[✓]		✓						
Twisting						✓		[✓]		✓		
Turning				✓		✓		✓		✓		
Balancing		[✓]		✓		✓		[✓]		✓		[✓]
Jumping		✓		✓				✓		✓		

Key: [✓] a main emphasis in the lesson   ✓ an emphasis in the lesson

All three aspects of each activity, i.e. composing, performing and appreciating in dance, and planning, performing and evaluating in gymnastics, should be apparent in every lesson.

Assessment

This should relate directly to the overall aims of the unit and the specific objectives for each lesson.

Dances within unit

Lessons 1–3   Space invaders
♪ *Accompaniment:* No 10 on the cassette
Resources: None required
Lessons 4–6   Spaghetti
♪ *Accompaniment:* Voice and percussion or
No 11 on the cassette
Resources: Poem 'Spaghetti' by Noel Petty (see page 121); uncooked spaghetti

Gymnastics within unit

Lessons 1–6   Curved and straight body shape
Twisting and turning

Year 5: Cross-curricular links (Key Stage 2)

Art / music

- Look at the way in which artists such as Miro, Klee and Kandinsky use patterns in their work. Try to recreate a musical pattern based on one of the above.

Art

- Look at repeat patterns in fabrics. Use these as a stimulus for fabric printing.
- Look at pattern and shape in buildings and develop a design from a window or a doorway.

Mathematics

- Find ways of measuring curved lines. Use X and Y axes to produce curve stitching.
- Measure the angles produced when lines meet or cross each other.

Food technology / maths

- Find a recipe for spaghetti bolognaise. Cost and purchase the ingredients and make the dish for a given number of people.

Geography

- Explain why roads and railways do not always take the shortest route between the places they link.

Science

- Investigate the action of heat on everyday materials resulting in a permanent change of state.

English

- Make shape or concrete poems using 'Spaghetti' by Noel Petty as an example.

Space invaders

Spaghetti

Movement emphasis — pattern using curving/ linear pathways

Year 5:
Lesson plans for dance

Space invaders

Dance framework

With an emphasis on linear formations and pathways, compose a dance for four people to include:

1 Individual sequence of sideways travel, explode, fall, roll and stand.

2 Ways of meeting, parting and avoiding each other.

3 Canon and unison.

Year 5

Lesson 1

Space invaders

Lesson 1

A Introduction

Galloping sideways pattern:

8 right   8 left

4 right   4 left

2 right   2 left

1 right   1 left

1 right   1 left

B Movement exploration and development

1 'On the spot, imagine being shot – emphasise the first sudden movement and then slow-motion falling to the floor.' Practise several times.

2 'Add a slow-motion roll to your fall.'

3 'Practise standing from the roll to begin the sequence again – explode, slow fall, roll and stand.'

4 Talk about the idea of space invader machines. Discuss the way the targets move across the screen, the pathways they make and the way they explode or disintegrate when they are hit.

5 'Practise moving sideways:

a galloping

b slow, large steps, bending knees

c quick, small steps

d any other ways of moving sideways on your feet.'

'How will your arms move as you are travelling?'

6 'Make a phrase of sideways steps, slow-motion hit, fall, roll and stand. Practise this going from right to left to right, remembering to keep all the movements on the same straight pathway.'

C Dance

With a partner, A does his/her sequence and B begins his/her sequence as A does the slow-motion hit. Each does his/her sequence three times, increasing the speed of the steps and the standing up, but keeping the hit and fall in slow motion. Finish with both A and B exploding at the same time.

D Conclusion

Any relaxation exercise.

Year 5
Lesson 2
Space invaders

Lesson 2

A Introduction

1 'Practise the galloping sequence from last lesson.'

2 'Practise the individual phrase you did – travel sideways, hit, fall, roll and stand.'

3 'Practise this with your partner, working in canon.'

B Movement exploration and development

1 'Run, dodging and swerving anywhere in the room. Go as close as you can to other people, ensuring that you do not touch them.'

2 Repeat 1 adding 'Turn away sharply from anyone you meet. You might include a small jump as you turn.'

3 Discuss the way that the targets are sometimes hit and what happens to them, i.e. they explode or disintegrate, but remind the children that the missiles sometimes miss their targets or the targets take evasive action.

'Try some of these ideas with a partner. Practise running towards a partner and
a explode
b go around each other
c go under and over each other.'

C Dance

'With a partner, make a dance to include:
a the phrase of sideways travel, hit, fall, roll and stand
b ways of meeting and avoiding, passing each other as practised in the movement exploration
c canon and unison.'

D Conclusion

Show and discuss some of the dances.

Year 5
Lesson 3
Space invaders

Lesson 3

A Introduction

1 Recap individual sequences.

2 Discuss some of the possibilities of working in fours to make a dance based on Space invaders, e.g.

- targets moving in canon and unison
- missiles moving in canon and unison
- three moving as targets with one as a missile
- two moving as targets with two as missiles
- one moving as a target with three moving as missiles
- all moving as targets
- all moving as missiles.

B Movement exploration and development

Try out some of these ideas.

C Dance

Compose a dance in fours, as outlined in the framework.

D Conclusion

Show and discuss the dances.

Spaghetti

Dance framework

1 Start in a linear shape away from partner. Using linear pathways:

   a meet partner

   b use follow my leader to travel and then copy each other's still shapes

   c make an extended linear shape in contact with each other.

2 Travel to finish in a four to make a linear group structure.

3 Using twisting and turning and curving, spiralling pathways, travel showing some of the various combinations possible when working in a four.

4 Finish in a 'fearful tizz' whether alone, in pairs, a trio or in a group of four.

Year 5

Lesson 4

Spaghetti

Lesson 4

A Introduction

'Run anywhere in the room using straight pathways. On a signal, stop in a linear shape.' Encourage the use of both horizontal and vertical lines and the use of different body parts to support weight, e.g. shoulders, backs, fronts, as well as feet.

B Movement exploration and development

1 'Find examples of straight lines in the hall, e.g. windows, doors, chairs, stage blocks. Stand near any of these objects and make your body match the straight lines of the object. Look for another object, run in a straight line towards it and make your body match the lines of the new object.' Ensure that weight is not always on the feet in the still shape and that the children travel forwards, backwards, and sideways varying their speed and length of step. Repeat several times.

2 'Find a partner. Stand one behind the other. Using the idea of travelling and stopping in linear pathways and shapes, A leads and B follows. B must copy A's shape when you stop. Change over.' Repeat several times.

3 'Come back into a space and see if you can make a linear shape in contact with your partner.'

Show different examples. Notice the different points of contact and emphasise the tension in the body. Ask children to choose one of the examples they have seen and to try it.

4 'Make a phrase with your partner based on linear floor pathways and body shape. Start away from your partner, meet your partner, use follow my leader matching your partner's still shape, and use the idea of the extended linear shape made in contact with your partner.' Encourage the use of different speeds.

5 Drop some dry spaghetti on the floor and discuss with the children the patterns formed. Notice how the pieces cross each other. 'Join with another pair and explore the different linear shapes you can make together as a four, based on the patterns made by the spaghetti.' Encourage shapes in which lines cross and overlap, perhaps combining horizontal and vertical lines with weight supported on different body parts.

6 'Using linear pathways, decide how you will travel from the shape you have made with your partner to meet in your group of four. Will you all use the same way of travelling? Will you all travel and arrive in your group shape at the same time or one after the other?'

C Dance

'Practise the dance made so far – that is your partner sequence and travelling to meet in your group of four, finishing in a linear shape. Remember to hold your finishing position.'

D Conclusion

Look at and discuss some of the work produced.

Lesson 5

Before the lesson, read and discuss with the class the shape poem 'Spaghetti' by Noel Petty. Discuss the different properties of dry and cooked spaghetti.

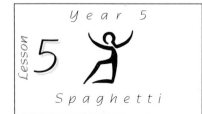

Year 5

Lesson 5

Spaghetti

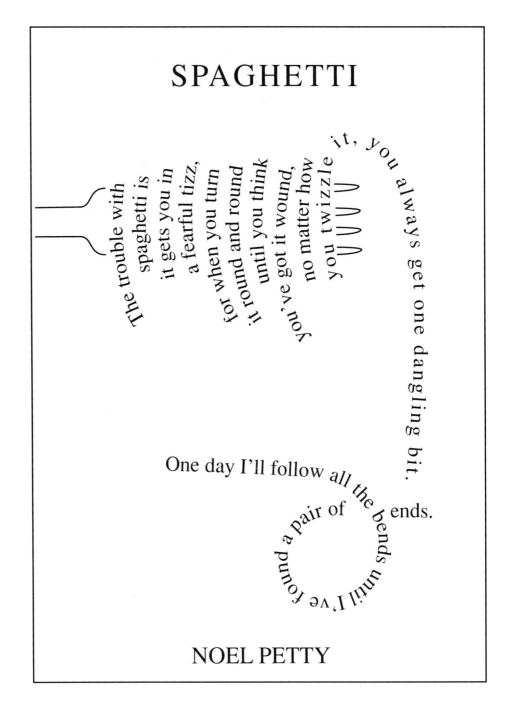

SPAGHETTI

The trouble with spaghetti is it gets you in a fearful tizz, for when you turn it round and round until you think you've got it wound, no matter how you twizzle it, you always get one dangling bit.

One day I'll follow all the bends until I've found a pair of ends.

NOEL PETTY

A Introduction

'Travel anywhere in the room using curving pathways. On a signal, settle in a curved shape. Use different parts of the body to lead the movement, e.g. elbows, shoulders, noses, wrists. See how smoothly you can let different parts of the body take over from each other to lead the movement.'

B Movement exploration and development

1 Remind the children of the poem which will have been introduced in the classroom. If you have an overhead projector, display the poem on a screen. Ask the children to copy a simplified pattern of the shape of the poem, using smooth running steps to trace it on the floor. E.g.

Remind them that they can travel backwards and sideways as well as forwards. Encourage the use of different body parts to lead the movement and the use of different levels.

2 Pick out some of the words in the poem which indicate turning movements, e.g. 'round and round', 'wound' and 'twizzle'. Ask the children to incorporate turns and spins into their floor pattern. Ensure that there are changes of speed in the phrase. Allow time for the children to practise.

3 Discuss with the children how they might interpret 'fearful tizz', e.g. they may show a twisted and tangled body shape. Ask the children to add their interpretation of the phrase to the end of their sequence of movement.

4 'Find the group with whom you worked last week. Stand one behind the other. The leader must take the group on a journey anywhere in the room using curving pathways.' Encourage twisting and spiralling pathways as well as curving and circular ones. Encourage the use of different levels, speeds and turning, spinning movements. Change over leaders frequently.

5 'Try the same idea in a line, but this time with hands joined.'

6 Experiment with the idea of getting the group into a 'fearful tizz'. Encourage the children to go through gaps made by each other's arms. Some of their movements may take them down to the floor. Change the leader frequently.

C Dance

'Starting with the linear group structure that you made last lesson, find ways of getting out of that structure which might have been produced by the pieces of dry spaghetti and into the various patterns that could be produced by the spaghetti as it is being cooked or twisted around a fork to be eaten. Use any of the ideas that we have worked on today and any other ideas of your own.

D Conclusion

Look at some of the work produced.

Year 5

Lesson 6

Spaghetti

Lesson 6

A Introduction

1 'Travel anywhere in the room using curving, spiralling pathways and curving spiralling movements, with different body parts leading.'

2 'Travel anywhere, using linear pathways. Remember to travel forwards, backwards and sideways. Pause in a linear body shape, before beginning to travel again.'

The rest of the lesson would be used to recap the sections of the dance, put them together, practise and view the results.

It would also be possible to use the stimulus of spaghetti in a different way – by concentrating on the movement qualities suggested by spaghetti, both in its cooked and uncooked states, i.e. brittle, sharp, sudden movements and smooth, continuous, fluid movements.

Year 5:
Lesson plans for gymnastics _____

Curved and straight body shape, twisting and turning

Year 5

Lesson 1

Twisting and turning

Lesson 1

A Warm-up

1 'Run around the hall and, when I say "Stop", freeze as still as a statue.'

2 'When I say "Stop", freeze close to the ground.'

3 'When I say "Stop", freeze stretched up as high as you possibly can.'

4 'When I say "Stop", you can choose which position you stop in.'

5 'Run and jump to make a straight-line shape in the air.'

B Floorwork

1 Show me a balanced position which is made up of straight lines, e.g.

Look at some examples and everyone try again.

2 'Do the balanced shapes all have to be high up or stretched up in the air? Could they be along the ground?' Possibilities include a star shape on the floor, lying on the floor. Look at the ideas and all try them.

3 'Choose two different straight-line balances on the floor and in the air and join them together like this:

  a Run to a space – balance (hold for 3 seconds)

  b Run to another space – balance (hold for 3 seconds)

  c Run to another space to jump high in the air to show straight lines in your body.'

4 'Can you turn your body in some way, still keeping your body in straight lines?' Possibilities include a log roll, spin, cartwheel.

Show some examples and let everyone try out the ideas.

C Apparatus

1 'Explore your apparatus by travelling in/out or under it.'

2 'Travel in/out/under/over and, when you come to a clear piece of apparatus, balance on it showing shapes made up of straight lines, as we did on the floor.'

3 'Can you travel between your apparatus using turns or spins showing straight lines in your body? Show examples of ideas and let the children try again.

4 'Can you now travel between the apparatus running, turning and spinning with your body in straight lines and then, when you come to a piece of apparatus, balance on it showing straight lines within your body? (Remember sometimes you can balance close to the apparatus and sometimes far away from it.) Can you jump from the apparatus before moving to the next piece?'

D Calming-down activity

'Take weight on hands with hips high in the air.'

<table>
<tr><td>Year 5</td></tr>
<tr><td>Lesson 2</td></tr>
<tr><td>Twisting and turning</td></tr>
</table>

Lesson 2

A Warm-up

'Practise running in and out of each other without making contact and, when you come to a clear space, show me any of the straight-line balances and the straight-line jumps that we did last lesson.' Show some examples to remind the children and then repeat the exercise.

B Floorwork

1 'Can you join together two straight-line balances with two straight-line turns or spins and a high jump?' Give the children time to compose a sequence of movements. Look at them and talk about linking movements together smoothly.

2 'Try again, concentrating on improving the transitions.'

3 'How can you turn or spin with your body in a curled shape?' Possibilities include forward rolls, sideways rolls, backward rolls, spin on bottom. Look at the ideas and teach any of the skills you think necessary to the whole class.

C Apparatus

1 'Travel in/out under apparatus avoiding contact with other people or apparatus.'

2 'Last lesson you travelled between the apparatus using turning and spinning. You then balanced on the apparatus before jumping off it. All these actions were done with the body in straight lines. Practise some of these ideas.'

3 'On your own piece of apparatus, is there any way you can roll or spin on it or from it with your body in a curled-up shape?' Look at some ideas and let everyone try again.

D Calming-down activity

'Trot – jump in the air and make a good landing.'

Year 5

Lesson

3

Twisting and turning

Lesson 3

A Warm-up

1 'Get out the mats and spread them around the hall. Run in and out of the mats.'

2 'Run in and out of the mats and, when you come to a clear one, jump over it or over a corner showing good straight lines in your body.'

3 'Can you run in and out of the mats and, when you come to a clear one, show some curled-up turns and spins from last lesson?'

B Floorwork

1 'Working on your own mat, jump high into the air to land on your mat, bend your knees to sink down and do a curled-up turn or spin.' Could be a jump into a forwards roll; a turning jump into a backwards roll; a quarter turn jump into a sideways roll or a jump, land, sink down and spin on bottom.

2 'Can you make a twisted, jagged, angular-shaped balance on the floor?' Here you can help guide the children by explaining that, if they have two or more different parts of their bodies on the floor, the other parts can twist away from them to make a twisted balance.

Look at ideas and let everyone try again – remember, bodies must be very tight and tense to hold the positions.

3 'Can you find three different twisted positions and join them together? You could have a position where your tummy is facing the floor or a position where your back is facing the floor or one where your side is facing the floor.'

Look at some ideas – remember tight bodies and good 'joins' between the different balances.

C Apparatus

1 'Travel in/out/under apparatus without making contact with anyone else or the apparatus.'

2 'Can you find any way of sliding down from your apparatus and turning or spinning away?' Look at some ideas and let everyone try again.

3 'Can you jump from any low pieces of apparatus, land and turn or spin away?'

4 'Can you hold a twisted balance on or against the apparatus?'

D Calming-down activity

'Travel round the hall and roll or spin in different ways.'

Lesson 4

A Warm-up

1 'Run into a space and show me a twisted balance, then run to another space and show another.'

2 'Can you remember how your twisted balances were joined together?' Give the children some minutes to remember and practise them.

B Floorwork

1 'Can you show me a twisted shape in the air? Let the children experiment with twisted jumps, then remind them that they can take off from either one foot or two feet. Look at some ideas and all try again.

2 'Can you do a twisted shape in the air, land, sink down and turn or roll away?' Look at some ideas.

3 'Can you now take your three twisted balances and join them together with twisted jumps and turns or rolls?' Allow time for experimentation, look at ideas and then give more time to work on their own sequences. Show sequences.

C Apparatus

1 'Travel in/out/under apparatus without making contact with anyone else or the apparatus.'

2 'Run in/out of apparatus and, when you come to a clear piece, balance on it, under it or against it showing a twisted body shape. Hold it for a count of 100/200/300 and then move on to another piece.'

3 'Move on to your own piece of apparatus. Can you hold a twisted balance on, against or under the apparatus and then either jump or roll out of it?' Look at some ideas, e.g. balance, slide, roll, and try again. Move round on the apparatus.

D Calming-down activity

'Travel backwards using different methods of moving.' It is essential to tell children that no one should run backwards and that when walking backwards, they should look over their shoulder to see where they are going

Lesson 5

A Warm-up

1 'Get out the mats and put them around the room. Show me all the different jumps you can do.' Look at some examples and ask everyone to try again.

2 'Travel in and out of the mats, jump, land and roll or spin away.'

3 'Run in and out of the mats, jump, sink down and roll away and move straight into a twisted balance.' Look at some ideas and let everyone try again.

B Floorwork

1 In pairs, A jumps, lands and rolls into a twisted balance. B jumps, lands and rolls to make a combined twisted balance with A.

2 'Can you travel on to the mat from different directions? Can you make up the balance smoothly?' Look at some of the ideas and then work on it again.

3 When the children have perfected that sequence into a good twisted balance in twos, ask B to roll or spin out of his/her balance into another one followed by A, who combines with B in another twisted balance?

4 Practise the sequence until it is perfect. Show two sequences.

C Apparatus

1 'Run in/out/under apparatus without making contact with each other or with the apparatus.'

2 'Can you roll/turn/spin towards a piece of apparatus and hold a twisted balance on, against or under it? Show some examples.

3 'With your partner, can you work out how you can travel towards your apparatus using jumps and rolls/turns/spins and hold a combined twisted balance on the apparatus?'

4 'In pairs, can you make a sequence with two combined twisted balances?'

D Calming-down activity

'Can you make a "bridge" position with your tummy facing the floor and then with your tummy facing the ceiling?'

Year 5

Lesson 6

Twisting and turning

Lesson 6

A Warm-up

1 'Show me all the different ways you can slide along the floor.'

2 'Show me all the different ways you can travel on hands and feet.'

3 'Show me all the different jumps you can do.'

B Floorwork

1 'Get out the mats. Run, jump, roll on a mat and make a twisted balance.'

2 'Join together in groups of three. Can you make up a twisted balance with one person on a high level, one person on a medium level and one person on a low level?' Look at the ideas produced and remind the children about body tension.

3 'From that balance, if you are on the low level, see if you can slide or roll through the balance held by the other two.' Practise this, i.e. balance in groups of three (count 100/200/300); the low-level child slides under and then runs and jumps on to another space to hold a balance; the other two follow to make a balance in a three again, this time with a different child on the low level. Practise this several times and then the low-level child slides under the other two to move to another spot to start the third and last balance.

4 Give the children plenty of time to practise and then show some examples of sequences.

C Apparatus

1 'Travel in/out/under apparatus without making contact with anyone or with apparatus.'

2 'Can you slide or roll underneath different parts of the apparatus?'

3 'In your group of three, on your own apparatus make a combined twisted balance with everyone on a different level.'

4 'When you have found a balance you like, try starting away from the apparatus and each other and work out a way of travelling towards the apparatus and going into your balanced position as smoothly as possible.'

5 'Can you travel towards the apparatus, hold the balance in your group and then slide/roll/spin away to hold a finishing position?'

D Calming-down activity

'Run around the hall and take up a bridge position, then run around again to take up another bridge position and so on.'

Work unit: Year 6

Aims of unit

To develop further:

a The concept of working with a partner
b Compositional skills.

Objectives	Lesson 1 Dance	Lesson 1 Gym	Lesson 2 Dance	Lesson 2 Gym	Lesson 3 Dance	Lesson 3 Gym	Lesson 4 Dance	Lesson 4 Gym	Lesson 5 Dance	Lesson 5 Gym	Lesson 6 Dance	Lesson 6 Gym
To increase the child's ability to show, use and identify												
a Some possibilities of working with a partner to include												
Action/reaction			☑								✓	
Meeting and parting	☑			✓	✓		✓			✓	✓	
Avoid by going around			☑	✓							✓	
Under and over each other			☑								✓	
Canon							☑	☑		☑	✓	☑
Synchronisation		☑		☑		☑		✓				✓
Different spatial relationships		✓			☑		☑		✓	✓	✓	✓
b Use of levels		✓	☑		✓		✓		✓			
c Rhythmic responses and phrasing	☑		☑		☑		✓		☑	✓	✓	✓
Through enlargement and the addition of basic actions enable the child to develop mimetic movement into dance	☑				✓		✓		✓		✓	

Key: ☑ a main emphasis in the lesson   ✓ an emphasis in the lesson

All three aspects of each activity, i.e. composing, performing and appreciating in dance, and planning, performing and evaluating in gymnastics, should be apparent in every lesson.

Assessment

This should relate directly to the overall aims of the unit and the specific objectives for each lesson.

Dances within unit

Lessons 1–6 A Fight – based on a painting by L. S. Lowry

♪ *Accompaniment:* 'Black and White Rag' (Theme tune for BBC television programme, *Pot Black*)

Resources: Lowry paintings, including 'A Fight' (1935)

Gymnastics within unit

Lessons 1–6 Synchronisation and canon

Year 6: Cross-curricular links (Key Stage 2)

History

- Put together information drawn from different historical sources, e.g. old newspapers, photographs and maps, to describe life in a local street in the 1930s. Compare this information with that gained from Lowry's paintings.
- Identify aspects of everyday life in Lowry's paintings, e.g. the role of women, family life, fashion, leisure, work, and see whether these have changed greatly or very little in today's world.

Art

- Draw or paint a picture based on an idea or theme depicted in one of Lowry's paintings.
- Compare the crowds of people in 'VE Day 1945' with those in Pieter Brueghel's 'Census at Bethlehem'.
- Discuss why Lowry painted people so simply.

English

- Describe some of the different characters seen in Lowry's paintings.
- Predict what might have happened just before and immediately after the scene in one of the paintings.

Music

- Compose two contrasting pieces based on two characters in any of the paintings.
- Listen to a jazz piece and identify solo instruments.

'A Fight' by L. S. Lowry

Year 6: Lesson plans for dance

A fight

Dance framework

Each to a count of eight:

Introduction – put on your hat.

1 Walk forwards, change front
2 Walk forwards, change front
3 Stand still – focus
4 Walk backwards, still focusing on same spot and meet partner
5 Advance and retreat with partner
6 Reverse this
7 Change places with partner
8 Repeat
9 Punches, action and reaction
10 Punches, action and reaction
11 Join both hands, twist and turn ⎫
12 In slow motion. ⎭

Sink down with partner.

1 A gets up and dusts him/herself off
2 A walks to new space
3 B does 1 and 2
4 to meet A
5 Arm wrestle in slow motion
6 Arm wrestle in slow motion
7 Change places with partner
8 Repeat
9 Meet partner and circle round them
10 *Schuhplattler*
11 Slow-motion twisting ⎫
12 and turning with partner ⎭

Sink down with partner.

Finish dance in own way – eight counts of eight.

Lesson 1

Before the lesson, the children should be familiar with some of L.S. Lowry's paintings.

A Introduction

1 a Jogging for eight counts, stretching for eight counts – repeat.

   b Jogging for eight counts, punching in different directions for eight counts.

2 Put **a** and **b** together.

B Movement exploration and development

Discuss how the people in some of Lowry's paintings might move, e.g. trudging along with hands in pockets, leaning forwards, kicking tin cans.

1 'Travel for eight counts bearing these ideas in mind.' Repeat several times. 'Can you add a run during your eight counts? Perhaps you trip over something so that you include some quick steps in your phrase.' Encourage different speeds, size of step and directions.

2 Hand out bowler hats. 'What difference does your hat make to your movement? How are you going to put it on – with one hand, or both hands?'

3 'Practise your travelling phrase changing your front after each eight counts.'

4 'Dance your phrase twice. Now stand still for eight counts, then walk backwards for eight counts.'

5 'When you are standing still, focus on something in the room and continue to focus on it as you travel backwards.'

Practise the 32 counts again, i.e. 1 – 4 of the dance framework.

6 'Find a partner. Go and stand together in a space in the room. This is where you will meet each other every time we do the dance. At the end of the travelling backwards phrase you will bump into your partner as you are so engrossed in whatever you are looking at. Decide how you will do this. Good, everyone rebounded off their partner.'

7 'For the next part of the dance you need to be close to your partner, so you will need to decide how you will meet each other after the rebound.' You could demonstrate with a pupil any of the ways in which the rebound has been performed and then ask the class to choose how they might meet their partner. Ask what might be a logical way and what might be more unexpected. This would also be an appropriate time to show some of the differences between dance and drama, e.g. adding an action of travel, turn and jump to any mimed movement.

Remind the class that there are associated actions which can extend any realistic movement. Any movement which normally is done on a forwards and backwards dimension, e.g. sawing, naturally lends itself to travelling forwards and backwards. A movement which normally goes from high to low, or vice versa, e.g. hammering, can easily be developed by adding a jump, while side-to-side movements, e.g. sowing seeds, can be developed through using turning actions. In this particular dance situation, if each partner took a swinging punch at the other one, then spinning or turning quickly on the feet would probably result.

'Practise your own sequence with your partner.'

'Decide with your partner exactly when you are going to meet each other. You can use up to four counts from the travelling backwards phrase to rebound away from your partner and to meet again. Practise this.'

C Dance

Practise the first 32 counts of the dance, i.e. 1–4 of the dance framework.

D Conclusion

Any relaxation activity.

Lesson 2

A Introduction

1 'Gallop sideways to the right for eight counts, then to the left for eight, the right for four counts, left for four counts, then right for two counts, left for two counts, then right for one count and left for one count, and right for one and left for one.' Repeat several times using any lively music.

2 'Practise the solo part of the dance (i.e. 1-4 of the dance framework), imagining that your partner is there.'

3 'Recap with your partner the rebounding and meeting phrase.'

4 Perform 1-4 of the dance framework.

B Movement exploration and development

1 Show children the painting 'A Fight' by L.S.Lowry. This appears to show two men advancing and retreating in contact with each other. Using this as a starting point, encourage children to make their own phrase of advancing and retreating using 16 counts in all. 'You may not advance and retreat for more than four counts without changing direction.' Look at some of these ideas.

2 'How can you change places with your partner?' Establish that you can avoid your partner by passing each other or by going under and over each other. Ideas such as leap-frogging over each other, or one performing a dive forwards roll while the other jumps over the top, might be suggested by the children. Draw on their work done in gymnastics lessons.

'You have 16 counts in which to do this, so that you will be able to change places more than once.' Experiment.

'Listen to the music and ensure that your movements fit.' Practise.

3 'Come and sit down.' Select a child to be your partner. Stand at arm's length from the pupil and ask him/her, without moving from the spot, to pretend to punch you. You do not react. Ask the class what is wrong with your response and encourage suggestions as to what you might do, e.g. duck, jump backwards or dodge. You then pretend to punch the pupil. Each action/reaction movement will take four counts so that the class will need to find four such examples that move logically from one to another.

C Dance

Practise 1 to 10 of the framework.

D Conclusion

Evaluate the work done so far by looking at some of the dances.

Year 6

Lesson 3

A fight

Lesson 3

A Introduction

1 Repeat as Lesson 2.

2 Recap the dance learned so far.

B Movement exploration and development

1 'Face your partner and join both hands with your partner. Without releasing your hold, experiment in slow motion how you can twist and turn.' Encourage the use of different levels and different relationships with the partner. 'Work out a sequence which lasts for 16 counts.'

2 At the end of 16 counts experiment with ways of sinking down to the floor. Remind them of the work done in gymnastics on counterbalance.

3 Practise the dance from the punching action and reaction section.

C Dance

1 Practise and perform the whole dance produced so far.

2 'Find another pair and sit down. You are going to show each other your dances. The pair watching will look for ways of improving the performance of the dancers. Do the movements follow continuously and smoothly? Which part do you like best and why? Discuss with the dancers how they can improve their dance. Dance it again with the improvements in mind.'

'Was it better this time?'

Change over with the other pair dancing. (Go through the same process, then share some of the dances with the whole class.)

D Conclusion

Any relaxation exercise.

Year 6

Lesson 4

A fight

Lesson 4

A Introduction

Practise the dance learned so far.

B Movement exploration and development

1 'In the next part of the dance A gets up and dusts him/herself off, travels to another space and freezes in a nonchalant position. B then does the same to confront A.'

'Everyone experiment with how you are going to get up. You might jump up, or spin around your hand and push yourself up or you may roll on to hands and feet before standing up. You decide.'

2 'Show me how you are going to dust yourself down, then travel to your new space and freeze. You can use any of the travelling ideas you have already used or make up some new ones.'

3 'Decide, with your partner, in what position A is going to freeze. For example, A might be leaning on a wall or reading a newspaper. How is B going to approach A? Will B approach him from the front or from behind? Is A aware of

B approaching or not? You have 16 counts each for this part of the dance, that is, getting up, dusting yourself down and travelling.'

4 'When you have confronted each other, the fight begins again. Face your partner and grasp each other's right hand. Try slow-motion arm wrestling. Change hands. You might force your partner on to the ground, then spin your partner round. You have 16 counts for this section.'

5 Put 3 and 4 together and practise.

6 'You remember how you changed places with your partner earlier in the dance, you now repeat this part of the dance. You may wish to keep it exactly the same as before or you may wish to alter it slightly. For example, you may change parts or you may change the order of the movements.'

C Dance

'Put together all the sections we have made today' (i.e. 1 to 8 in the second half of the framework).'

D Conclusion

Any relaxation exercise.

Year 6

Lesson 5

A fight

Lesson 5

A Introduction

'Practise the dance beginning from where you sank on to the floor with your partner.'

B Movement exploration and development

1 'Instead of repeating the action/reaction punching section of the dance, perhaps we could alter it slightly.' Show the class a simple *schuhplattler* fight, i.e. face partner – A pretends to slap B with his/her right hand while B ducks slightly to his/her own right, clapping both hands by his/her right side. B then pretends to slap A and A claps his/her hands. While the children are practising, they will probably need to take eight counts to complete the whole of the above. Some children may pick this up very quickly and need only four counts for the sequence, so they can repeat it again. Practise this.

2 'After you have changed places with your partner you will have eight counts before the *schuhplattler* phrase. Perhaps you could advance towards your partner and circle around each other as if sizing up each other.' Practise.

3 Put together 2 and 1 (i.e. 9 and 10 in the second half of the framework).

4 'After this section you repeat the twisting and turning section for 16 counts and sink down together as before.'

C Dance

1 Practise 1 to 12 of the second half of the framework.

2 Practise the whole dance from the beginning.

D Conclusion

Watch and evaluate some of the dances.

Year 6

Lesson 6

6

A fight

Lesson 6

A Introduction

Recap the whole dance.

B Movement exploration and development

'Using any of the ideas we have worked on so far, or any new ideas, you have eight counts of eight in which to finish the dance in your own way.'

The rest of this lesson should be taken up with this, putting the whole dance together and viewing the results.

Year 6:
Lesson plans for gymnastics

Synchronisation and canon

Year 6

Lesson **1**

Synchronisation and canon

Lesson 1

A Warm-up

1 'Can you travel in and out of each other in as many different ways as possible?' Look at some of the ideas.

2 'Can you travel round the hall with the front part of your body facing towards the floor?' Show some examples and try out the ideas.

3 'Now can you travel round the room with your back towards the floor?' Show some examples and let everyone try out the ideas.

4 'Is it possible to travel round the room with your side towards the floor?' Look out for examples.

5 'Can you now travel round the room in different ways, but sometimes with your body the right way up and other times with your body upside down in relation to the floor?'

B Floorwork

1 'Remembering all the different ways, travel round the room constantly changing your mode of travelling. When I say "Stop" hold your position.

'Now let's all start at the same time and finish at the same time.' Repeat the whole task several times.

2 Then ask:

'Were you all doing the same movement?' – 'No'

'Were you all travelling in the same direction?' – 'No'

'Were you all moving and stopping at the same time?' – 'Yes'

Establish that starting and finishing at the same times is *synchronisation*. Use the example of synchronising watches, i.e. checking that they are showing precisely the same time.

3 'Find a partner. Perform a movement side by side, where you start at the same time and finish at the same time.' Allow experimentation. Use examples to see if partners are starting and finishing at the same time as each other. Look at some of the synchronised movements and discuss their effectiveness.

C Apparatus

1 'Explore the apparatus individually – under/along/over/through it.'

2 'Travel over/under/along/through the apparatus and along the floor, never stopping and having different parts of your body facing the apparatus.'

3 'In pairs, stand on opposite sides of the apparatus. Start at the same time and arrive on the apparatus at the same time.' Use examples to show 'good' synchronisation.

D Calming-down activity

'Travel in several ways with hands on the floor only.'

<table>
<tr><td>Year 6</td></tr>
<tr><td>Lesson 2</td></tr>
<tr><td>Synchronisation and canon</td></tr>
</table>

Lesson 2

1 'Remembering what we did last lesson, can you move in and out of each other, travelling round the hall with different parts of your body facing the floor? Remember you can have your back, front, or side facing the floor and you can be upside down or the right way up.'

2 'In pairs, side by side, travel round the hall; keep together, but you need not necessarily do the same movement.'

B Floorwork

1 'Can you perform a jump side by side in synchronisation?' Show examples of children doing different jumps at the same time as each other.

2 'With a partner, find a starting position side by side and work out how you can perform two different travelling movements each, to start and finish at the same time as each other.' Allow time for experimentation, then look at some examples. Try again. Show an example of good synchronisation.

Children should, by now, have worked out their timing precisely. Ask whether they have to stand side by side to perform their sequence? You should establish that the answer to this is no – they could start together and move away from each other, start apart and move towards each other or they could start fairly close and pass by each other, etc. Try some ideas and examples of the more successful ones.

C Apparatus

1 'Explore the apparatus individually – over/under/along/through it.'

2 'Can you travel on to the apparatus hands first?' Show examples and then repeat the task. 'Can you travel from the apparatus hands first?' Show examples and try again.

3 'In pairs, can you put together two movements so that you start and finish at the same time as each other? Don't forget you can follow different pathways and use different levels.' Allow time for experimentation and then show some examples. (This task encourages sliding from the apparatus in different ways.)

D Calming-down activity

'Travel round the hall mixing high and low jumps with rolls and spins.'

<table>
<tr><td>Year 6</td></tr>
<tr><td>Lesson 3</td></tr>
<tr><td>Synchronisation and canon</td></tr>
</table>

Lesson 3

A Warm-up

1 'Run in and out of each other and jump high into a space. Remember to let your knees and ankles give in when you land.'

2 'Run in and out of each other and jump high into a space to sink down and finish in a crouched position.' Choose an example to illustrate the controlled sinking down.

3 'Run and jump into a space, sink down and sideways roll away.' Repeat several times. Look at someone performing the sink and roll very smoothly.

B Floorwork

1 'Find a partner and perform your sequence of run, jump and sideways roll side by side. Try to begin and finish at the same time.' Look at some examples, if possible, of two children performing different jumps and two children performing the same jump. Emphasise the point that they started at the same time and finished at the same time, even though one pair was doing the same jump and the other was not.

2 'With your partner, perform the sequence you composed last lesson, but now can you add a travelling movement or jump and roll, ensuring that you start and finish at the same time as each other? Try to do similar movements to your partner's.'

C Apparatus

1 'Explore your apparatus individually – over/under/along/through it.'

2 'Can you remember the movements where you travelled on to the apparatus with hands first and travelled away with hands leading?' Show some examples to remind them of the different ideas.

3 'With your partner, put together two movements where you are working in synchronisation, starting at the same time and finishing at the same time, and one movement, with hands leading, where you are working together doing similar movements.'

D Calming-down activity

'Take long slow steps around the hall, then pivot on toes before continuing with long slow steps, etc.'

Year 6

Lesson 4

Synchronisation and canon

Lesson 4

A Warm-up

1 'With a partner, side by side, trot around the room in and out of other people, avoiding contact.'

2 'Change the way you travel on your feet, still side by side with your partner.'

3 'Stand side by side – A chooses a spot on the floor and runs and jumps to land on it. When A has landed, B runs and jumps to land on a spot beside A'. Repeat this several times.

B Floorwork

1 'Individually, trot in and out of each other and jump into a space when you see one. Remember to show different shapes in the jumps.' Choose some different shapes – show them – give teaching points and let all the children try them out.

2 'As a pair, decide on a favourite jump and practise it so you can start and finish precisely at the same time as each other, performing the same jump together.' Show examples of several pairs performing well.

3 Choose a pair and watch A perform the jump, followed closely by B. Establish with the children that this is not synchronisation. The pair performed similar movements, but one after the other in *canon* (as in singing a round or canon).

4 Compose a sequence made up of two synchronised movements and one canon movement.

C Apparatus

1 'Individually, explore your apparatus – over/under/along/through it.'

2 'Stand side by side with your partner on the apparatus – can you jump off in canon, showing different shapes in the air?'

3 'Can you dismount in any other way in canon?' Choose some examples; perhaps show sets of canon using the same movements and sets using different movements.

D Calming-down activity

'Run sideways round the hall, sometimes tucked up and sometimes straight.'

Year 6

Lesson **5**

Synchronisation and canon

Lesson 5

A Warm-up

1 'How can you travel round the room on your feet?'

2 'Show me all the different ways you can travel on different parts of your body.'

3 'Travel round in different ways changing direction, sometimes travelling forwards, sometimes backwards, sometimes sideways.'

4 'Can you sometimes travel high and sometimes low?'

B Floorwork

1 'Stand side by side and show me your jumps in canon – the ones we did last lesson.'

2 'Can you keep repeating these, but in rhythm?' Emphasise this important point about canon – children should move rhythmically one after the other.

3 'With your partner, make a sequence of two travelling movements and one jump, performing the individual movements in canon. Remember you can use different directions.' Look at some examples. Ask children if rhythm is the binding factor of canon, does this mean that canon movements have to be the same as each other? Emphasise that two movements performed in canon need not necessarily be the same movements, but they must take up the same amount of time in order to maintain the rhythm.

4 'Go back to your sequence and alter one of your sets of canon movements so you are performing different movements.'

C Apparatus

1 'Explore the apparatus individually.'

2 'How can you travel on to your apparatus? How can you travel from your apparatus?'

3 'With a partner, travel towards the apparatus in canon, travel on to it in canon and travel from the apparatus in canon.' Look at some examples.

D Calming-down activity

'Run side by side with a partner avoiding every other pair in the hall – change pace.'

Year 6

Lesson

6

Synchronisation and canon

Lesson 6

A Warm-up

1 'Travel round the hall on your feet.'

2 'Travel round the hall with your feet higher than your head.'

3 'Travel round the hall moving your weight from feet to hands and back to feet again.'

4 'Stand side by side with a partner. Call yourselves A and B. When I call out your letter you travel, jump, roll – any movement you wish – into a space and stop.' You should slowly and rhythmically call out A and B, and A and B, etc. Keep the rhythm going – children can travel in any direction and they need not be near their partner.

B Floorwork

1 Put together two sets of canon jumps and one synchronised or unison travelling movement. Have good starting and finishing positions. Look at sequences.

2 Two pairs join together to make a four. Put a hoop in a space.

3 'One after the other, jump into the hoop on to two feet and jump straight out again.'

4 'Can you now jump in and out of the hoop in rhythm (1 and 2 and 3 and 4 – repeat)?'

5 'When you get the rhythm right, can you jump into it from different directions and out of it in different directions? Make up patterns.' Show some examples.

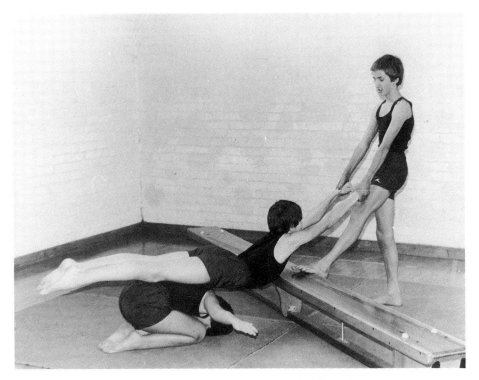

'Approach the apparatus in canon, synchronise to hold a balance.'

C Apparatus

1 'Explore the apparatus individually – over/under/along/through it.'

2 'In pairs, can you approach the apparatus and get on it in canon?' Show some examples.

3 'Approach the apparatus and get on it in canon, use the apparatus in synchronisation and then dismount in canon.' Allow time to complete the sequences and then look at them.

D Calming-down activity

'Roll, balance, roll about the hall.'

C Apparatus

5 Cross-curricular Projects

The two projects that follow are further examples of the way that dance and gymnastics can enhance each other and other curriculum areas. The first was based on landscape and the environment, with work in science providing the initial stimulus, while the second project was developed from work in gymnastics on counterbalance and countertension.

Landscape

As has already been said, the idea of an integrated curriculum is not to use one medium to teach another, but rather to encourage the children to use all their senses to experience the world through a multitude of viewpoints, with one area of the curriculum stimulating or reinforcing work in others. This was certainly the case with a project based on landscape and the environment which was undertaken with a class of 9- to 11-year-olds.

The project was initiated by work undertaken in science and the work centred particularly on enabling the children 'to describe from their observations some of the effects of weathering on buildings and on the landscape'. It was also concerned with the different properties of various materials and with the children's understanding of 'the sequence of changes which result from heating and cooling'.

These were the starting points, but the project soon developed a life of its own, encompassing far more than had initially been envisaged and soon covered most aspects of the curriculum with help from advisory teachers, parents and an artist in residence. The focus here, however, will be on the art, dance and gymnastics work, since these were the areas in which the authors were most directly involved.

At the outset of the project, the children were encouraged to observe the shape, pattern, colour and texture of the environment surrounding the school. This stimulated the children to make torn paper landscape pictures using a variety of textured papers. If the children could not find the 'right' paper, in terms of

colour or texture for their pictures, they made their own by printing, diffusing or dipping and dyeing.

This attention to detail was further developed by the visiting artist – a sculptress who shared her work and ideas with the children. She helped the class to make wall hangings, again inspired by the textures and autumnal colours of the local environment. Armed with six sheets of sugar paper in greens, rusts, browns and yellows, the children took rubbings from different surfaces in the school playground. These included brickwork, fences, trees, utility covers and the surface of the playground itself. All the sheets were then placed on top of one another and holes were formed in the paper by tearing to reveal different colours and textures beneath. The holes were enlarged and decorated by spiralling, coiling and weaving wools around and across the holes, inspired by the textures of the rubbings on the paper.

The idea was extended to make a large three-dimensional hanging using six layers of hessian, but this time, space was allowed between each layer enabling the children to walk between them. This hanging was also different from the paper hangings because of the different properties of the material used. It could be textured through the use of embroidery and it could also be frayed to produce fringes which could be left free or woven.

The artist's own work was also a source of inspiration for the children. They were able to touch and handle examples of the work she brought with her. Two pieces of work, in particular caused much interest. Both were based on organic forms – one made from metal and the other from latex. Through the use of slides and discussion with the artist, the children were able to understand how, by heating, a square, flat piece of metal could be changed in colour, shape and texture into a three-dimensional sculpture full of positive and negative spaces.

The different properties of the latex were experienced at first hand with the children making their own organic forms, based on objects they had found in the environment.

The dance

All these visual and tactile experiences enabled the children to bring a wealth of additional ideas and understanding to the dance that was eventually created. This was based on a poem 'The Land' by Celia Mayes and evolved over a period of six weeks.

Ideally, the teacher of any subject should be a facilitator and guide with whom the children discuss their ideas. The teacher then asks pertinent questions to allow the children to develop further their work. This is ideal for children who have a reasonable background and experience within the area involved and have a wealth of ideas on which to draw, but it is very difficult if this is not the case.

This is particularly so in dance. To ask children to create a dance without any knowledge of the language of movement or composition is likely to be a recipe for disaster, especially if the children are aged 9 and above. Some of the more confident children and those with natural body facility may achieve something that approximates to dancing, but whether or not they would be able to compose a dance would be debatable. This is not to say that when teaching dance children must slavishly imitate steps and phrases imposed on them by the teacher, but rather that a framework for the dance is produced to give sufficient security and structure for everyone to benefit (see chapter 3). A structure may be provided by the teacher and firmed up with the children or the structure may be produced by the teacher and children together.

Since the children involved in this project had little or no previous dance experience, the advisory teacher for dance had devised a loose compositional structure for the dance based on different sections of the poem as shown opposite and on page 148.

She had also thought about the movement possibilities suggested by the poem. These thoughts and ideas were in no way written on tablets of stone and were constantly being revised according to the responses and suggestions of the children.

We began by reading the poem together and discussed the feelings that the poem evoked. What smells and sounds would be evident in such a landscape? What colours would you see? What would it feel like to touch this environment?

We then looked at the poem in the sections indicated, concentrating on the movement possibilities suggested by each one. The class was asked to describe how the molten metals might move. The children's suggestions included flowing fluidly, rolling, cascading, slithering, covering and erupting. How could those be translated into movement? Most of these words already had action and dynamic qualities inherent within them and some of them were used as a stimulus for improvised movement.

It was eventually decided that smooth rolling and spinning movements with the body constantly changing from rounded to elongated shapes would best interpret the idea of the molten metals. These movements were then interspersed with sudden jagged shapes made by gestures of the arms, legs or the whole body as the metal spluttered and erupted across the earth's surface. Movements generally were kept at a low or medium level, although some children did choose to use jumps to symbolise the eruptions, but the focus of the jumps was always directed towards the earth.

The Land

Section 1 A hundred thousand million years ago
The land was hot
and empty;
Covered

Section 2 By molten metals, and the
Sluggish sea, crawling over
slow-cooling granite

Section 3 And from the barren skin of
Ancient shapes, the mighty Sculptor
Carved out valleys, raised up
Crumbling hills, and

Section 4 Broke them
Violently apart, lifting fiery fountains
from the sea.
Then
Were many mighty mountains made;

Section 5 And the wrinkled skin of land
Still lies, pitted
And disfigured;
Ever changing.

by Celia Mayes

Eventually each child made his/her own phrase of smooth weight transference punctuated by sudden angular shapes which either accelerated to finish suddenly or decelerated to peter out. Throughout the phrase, the shapes that the body made were emphasised, whether these were rounded, elongated, jagged or sometimes using an amalgam of several at the same time. Words such as devouring, engulfing, covering and surrounding intensified the quality and clarity of the movements produced by the class.

The children suggested that at least two people would need to work together to interpret the second section of the poem so that the sluggish sea actually had something to crawl over. This is not to say that in any way the children were pretending to be the sea, but rather that they were abstracting the essence of the way the sea might move and interpreting this in their own bodies by the use of appropriate actions and dynamic and spatial qualities. In this section of the dance, they also had to think about the relationship with their partner or partners.

The children had already drawn quite strongly on their knowledge of gymnastics in section 1 of the dance, in which they had used a great deal of rolling and spinning in their transference of weight. Their gymnastics experience was even more evident in section 2 of the dance, when the children suggested that they could use some of the ideas they had discovered during their gymnastics lessons on the theme of holes and barriers, to interpret the dance idea. During the gymnastics sessions the children had worked in pairs, travelling under, over and around their partner. Sometimes the partner had been stationary in a balanced position, such as a bridge, while at other times the partner had had to negotiate a moving obstacle with both partners moving at the same time. Sometimes physical contact was made as children slid or leap-frogged over each other and at others it was avoided. Sequences of movement had been made by the children so that each partner alternated between negotiating the obstacle and becoming the obstacle to be negotiated.

It was some of these ideas which were recalled and adapted for section 2 of the dance. The gymnastics ideas and skills were not, however, lifted wholesale and merely reproduced in the dance situation. The movements were chosen because of their appropriateness in conveying the dance idea and not merely to show the skills of body management. Obviously, skills of performance are very important in dance since lack of such skills can obscure the communication of the intended idea. In dance, however, the ultimate concern is with the meaning of the movement and its expressive quality rather than with its purely practical function.

The gymnastics skills used in section 2 of the dance, therefore, were now adapted and used in a dance-like way. The shape of the body, both in stillness and motion, the dynamic and spatial features and the movements themselves were all chosen by the children because of their appropriateness in conveying the idea of the solidifying granite and the slow-moving sea.

Some of the children discovered that working in groups of three added other possibilities to develop the dance idea. Two children could now make gaps for the third to slither, slide, roll or jump through. One child could represent the 'slow-cooling granite' while the other two could completely surround or engulf it like the sea. One child could now slither from greater heights down the back of another, aided by the third member of the group. Sometimes two children broke away from the third as if a piece of the granite had solidified, while the sea surged on.

The children decided that they would need to work in larger groups to represent the idea of 'carved out valleys' and 'crumbling hills' so that the third section of

the dance was concerned with twos and threes meeting together and the formation of larger group shapes.

Seeing the works produced by the sculptress and her practical work with the children had considerably influenced their understanding of the ways that materials behaved both in liquid and solid states. This understanding had also fuelled their imagination influencing the quality of the movements produced in sections 1 and 2 of the dance. They knew about molten metals and the solidifying of the latex and these visual and tactile images served to stimulate their senses and to enhance their dance both in terms of ideas and the quality of movement produced.

Similarly, the children's previous observation of the shape, pattern and texture in the landscape served to make them more visually aware and critical when producing their group shapes in section 3 of the dance. The children experimented making different shapes – curved, linear, angular, representing sometimes gentle rolling countryside and sometimes dramatic mountainous formations. Children took it in turns to stand outside their own group to look at what they had produced to see if it was visually interesting. Was the group all on the same level? Was everyone facing in the same direction? Was everyone standing? Might it be more effective if weight were not always on feet? Was the group too close together? Were there any gaps in the overall shape? Were these accidental? If they were intentional did they need to be even more defined? There were obviously no correct answers to these questions, but rather they were asked to help the children to clarify their ideas and to make their intentions clear in visual terms.

The final problem to be solved in this section of the dance was that of the actual formation of the group. Who needed to get into position first? In what order did the other dancers need to arrive? Might they want to arrive all at the same time or one after the other? What movements would be used by each dancer to travel into the formation? Answers having been found to these questions, section 4 of the dance was discussed. The predominant movement qualities already used in the dance had been sustained and strong, interspersed with some sudden movements and moments of stillness. It was felt, therefore, that energetic sudden movements would give contrast to the dance and such movements would also be very appropriate for the violent breaking apart of the 'crumbling hills' and 'carved out valleys'. Contrast would also be provided by the jumps which were suggested by the idea of 'fiery fountains' being lifted from the sea.

It was at this point that more attention was given to the accompaniment to be used for the dance. Until now the words of the poem and percussion had been used, but it was suggested that a piece of atmospheric music might also add to the mood of the dance. The piece of music chosen and accepted by the class also had a rhythmic section which it was felt would be ideal for section 4 of the dance. The rhythm was clapped and stamped and played percussively on different parts of the body. It was marked on the spot and while travelling, using stepping and jumping. The rhythmic pattern was then used to break away from the group and reform elsewhere, either in the same or a contrasting formation to that created at the beginning of this section.

The dance was concluded by repeating the first section with its sustained, smooth rolling and turning movements, with the children either finishing alone or in contact with others if they had been encountered in their travelling sequence.

With the composition of the dance established, attention was again directed towards the accompaniment for it.

Atmospherically, the music and the dance matched each other well, but it was felt that the poem should be spoken at the same time as the music was played to make the accompaniment even more effective.

The rhythmic pattern of the music used in section 4 of the dance also needed strengthening to match the quality of the movements as the valleys and hills were violently broken apart. Percussion was therefore used for this purpose. Since the music had not been written specifically for the dance and neither had the dance been composed with the music as its stimulus, it was not surprising that these adjustments had to be made so that the accompaniment and the dance would complement each other as effectively as possible to make a whole.

The emphasis in this project was on the way that work in science, art, dance and gymnastics served to reinforce and stimulate each other in a particular project. One discipline was not more important than the others, but each had a high profile at various times during the project, while at others it had a more subsidiary role. Very important, however, were the cross-curricular links that were constantly being made, enabling the children to make connections and think across subject barriers.

The dance ideas have already been described in this chapter, but a more detailed outline of a proposed unit of work follows. This is only a suggestion to be used as a starting point for the dance idea. It would obviously need to be adapted, not only to the needs, aptitudes and experience of the children involved, but also according to the class's own ideas about the poem and therefore the dance. Similarly, a gymnastics scheme of work on the theme of holes and barriers is also included.

Work unit: Landscape

Aims of unit

To create a dance composition and gymnastic sequences incorporating work from other aspects of the curriculum.

Objectives	Lesson 1		Lesson 2		Lesson 3		Lesson 4		Lesson 5		Lesson 6	
	Dance	Gym	Dance	Gym	Dance	Gym	Dance	Gym	Dance	Gym	Dance	Gym
a To improve the child's ability to												
Enrich movements by varying shape, speed and level	✓	✓	✓	✓		[✓]		✓	✓	✓		✓
Increase the complexity of body actions and the use of body parts to take weight	✓	✓	✓	✓		✓		✓	✓	✓		
Repeat phrases/sequences of movement accurately	✓		✓	✓	✓	✓	✓		[✓]	[✓]		✓
Work in groups with a particular emphasis on making holes and barriers		[✓]	[✓]	[✓]		✓	✓	[✓]	✓			✓
b Group shapes	[✓]		✓		[✓]				✓			
A variety of jumps				[✓]			✓	✓	[✓]	✓		
Describe and interpret the different elements of a dance composition	✓		✓		✓		✓		[✓]			
Describe the different elements of a gymnastics sequence								✓		✓		✓

Key: [✓] a main emphasis in the lesson   ✓ an emphasis in the lesson

All three aspects of each activity, i.e. composing, performing and appreciating in dance, and planning, performing and evaluating in gymnastics, should be apparent in every lesson.

Assessment

This should relate directly to the overall aims of the unit and the specific objectives for each lesson.

Dances within unit

Lessons 1–5   Landscape
♪ *Accompaniment:*   No 12 on the cassette
   Resources: 'The Land' by Celia Mayes (see page 144)

Gymnastics within unit

Lessons 1–6   Holes and barriers

Lesson plans for dance

Landscape

Dance framework

1 Individual sequence – alternating between rounded and angular shapes, linked by travelling, turning and jumping. Finish by meeting in a group of three.

2 Trio – slither over and around each other through the gaps made by the group.

3 Finish by meeting another three to form an irregular group shape of six people.

4 Sextet – explosive jumping apart of the group which then reforms into another irregular group shape.

5 Individual sequence – as 1 above, finishing by slithering, spinning or rolling to meet in a group of three again, or alone.

Explosive jumping.

Lesson 1

A Introduction

1 'Travel anywhere in the room using a curving pathway – on a beat from the tambour, make yourself as small as possible'. Repeat several times.

2 'Do the same again, but this time, roll in your rounded shape. Jump up and begin again.'

B Movement exploration and development

1 'Show me a strong, jagged body shape. Remember how tense your body must feel. Show me another strong shape. Change the shape each time a beat is played on the tambour.'

2 'Show me a curved, rounded body shape. Try to make sure that there are no parts of your body making angular shapes. Change the shape each time a beat is played on the cymbal. Can you take your weight on different parts of the body to make the shape?'

3 'See if you can keep moving from a rounded shape into jagged shapes to the accompaniment.' Use either a tambour, tambourine or cymbal. Encourage:

   a transference of weight using different body parts

   b change of level

   c different body parts to initiate the movement

   d successive rather than simultaneous flow so that the movements ripple through the body.

4 'Make a travelling sequence or phrase moving in and out of curved and strong, jagged shapes – you could use rolls, spinning and turning, creeping and crawling or any other ideas you may have.'

   Read and discuss section 1 of the poem again, encouraging the children to describe how the molten metals might move. Some of the words could be used as an accompaniment for this section of the dance.

5 'Try your travelling sequence again. Perhaps you can say your words as you move. Make sure there are some changes of speed in your sequence. Does your sequence start slowly and get faster or does it build to a climax and slow down again? You choose.'

   Read and discuss section 2 of the poem.

6 'Decide how and where you will meet in your threes. Will you arrive at the same time or one after another? Will you be moving in the same way as your partners? What sort of combined shape will you make together to represent the solidifying granite?'

C Dance

'Link your individual sequence with meeting in your threes. Make your combined shape clear. Feel as if you are being drawn towards your partners.' Practise the whole phrase.

D Conclusion

Discuss the dance phrases produced. Were they effective? If so, why and if not, why not? Possibly look at some examples if this is appropriate.

Cross-curricular projects

Lesson **2**

Landscape

Lesson 2

A Introduction

'Practise the molten metal sequence you made in the last lesson. See how smoothly you can travel from one shape into another and then surprise me with some sudden movements.'

B Movement exploration and development

Read and discuss section 2 of the poem.

'Find the partners with whom you worked last week. Show me the combined shape you made together. See how you can slither around and over each other and through gaps created by the group.' For further ideas, see the gymnastics lessons on pages 153–6.

C Dance

Practise the dance made so far, i.e. sections 1 and 2 of the framework.

D Conclusion

1 Look at some examples of the work produced.

Cross-curricular projects

Lesson **3**

Landscape

Lesson 3

A Introduction

Anything involving stretching, curling and travelling.

B Movement exploration and development

Read and discuss section 3 of the poem.

1 'Find the partners with whom you worked last week. Join with another three to make a group of six. Number yourselves from one to six. All number ones make a rounded shape. Number twos, can you join on to your number one remembering to keep the overall shape rounded?' Eventually five children in each group make the rounded group shape, with the sixth member of the group acting as the choreographer. It is important that the group shape is not always formed in the same order and that each child has a turn at observing the group shape and acting as the choreographer.

2 'What sort of shapes are suggested by "valleys" and "crumbling hills"?' The same process can be used to make these group shapes as was used to make the rounded shapes. The shapes may be jagged and angular or they may combine both curved and angular features.

3 'Now you have tried out various possibilities for the group shapes, decide which one you are going to keep. What sort of dynamic qualities are suggested by the words "carved out" and "raised up"? How will these qualities be interpreted in the formation of the group? Who arrives first? Work out the order in which everyone else needs to arrive? Where will you all meet? What sort of movements are you going to use to travel to meet each other?'

C Dance

1 'Let's practise moving from your threes into the formations in your groups of six.'

2 'Practise your work in threes.' (Section 2 of the dance.)

3 'Let's put together your work in threes, travelling to meet the rest of your group and the formation of the "valleys" and "crumbling hills".' (Sections 2 and 3 of the dance.)

D Conclusion

Look at some examples of the work produced.

Lesson 4

A Introduction

1 'Show me how you can bounce on the spot. Can you bounce very close to the floor? Forwards and backwards? Side to side? Run and bounce into another space. Can you make a pattern of bounces, jumps and running from space to space? Include some very small bounces and some large explosive jumps.'

B Movement exploration and development

1 'Listen to this clapping rhythm and repeat it back to me.' Use the rhythmic pattern found in the music suggested or make up one of your own, if this accompaniment is not being used.

2 'Let's stamp the rhythm.'

3 'Using your hands, play the rhythm on different parts of your body.'

4 'Make the rhythm with different parts of the body moving. You might use your head, shoulders, hips, elbows, fingers, knees, etc.'

5 'Use the rhythm to make a travelling pattern. You could skip, jump, step, hop, etc.'

6 'Travel for part of the phrase and mark the other part on the spot, sometimes with percussive body sounds and sometimes in silence. You don't need to move all the time. You could pause for one or two beats.'

Read and discuss section 4 of the poem and the movement ideas it suggests.

C Dance

1 'In your sixes, use the rhythmic pattern we have worked on to create the violent breaking apart of the valleys and hills and the "lifting" of the "fiery fountains".' Encourage the use of canon and unison, turning, jumping, rising and falling.

2 'Make sure that your group reforms to create the "mighty mountains".'

3 'Starting from your finishing position in your threes, put together the travelling section you use to make your group of six (section 3) and then dance the rhythmic section you have just worked on (section 4).'

D Conclusion

Discuss and evaluate the work produced.

Lesson 5

A Introduction

1 'Let's clap the rhythmic pattern we used last week.'

2 'Show me how you can stamp it.'

3 'Show me how you can travel using the same pattern.'

The rest of this lesson would be used to recap the various sections of the dance, putting the sections together, practising them and viewing the results.

Gymnastics

Obviously, the dance and gymnastics schemes were running in the same term and each discipline drew upon the work of the other to complement and enhance both the understanding of the children, and their physical competence. Perhaps more emphasis was placed on the learning of the techniques for the safe performance of weightbearing movements in the gymnastics lessons than it was in dance lessons. The children were then able successfully to transfer and translate them into meaningful dance movements. Conversely, the qualities of fluidity and continuity developed in their dance lessons were used to excellent effect in the production of gymnastic sequences.

Initially, drawing on ideas from the art project, children were asked to describe the shapes which might be found in a landscape. Smooth, rolling, mountainous, flat, hilly were some of the words used. However, at this point, the children realised that a landscape could encompass more than mere terrain, and trees, bridges, rivers and human-built structures could also be included in the description of a landscape.

Having discussed the nature and composition of a landscape, the children first recalled work on balance in which they had previously been involved – balancing on different body parts to produce different shapes, sometimes jagged and twisted, sometimes smooth and rounded. Once these shapes had been recalled and practised, the children worked with a partner exploring ways of travelling beneath and around each other. Likening this to passing through tunnels, it was decided that the travelling had to be close to the ground so that slithering, sliding and rolling were used. The work was then developed with one partner holding a balance while the other travelled under and around him/her.

Tunnelling beneath and travelling around interesting shapes naturally developed into travelling over the balances. Here, the teacher initially invited the responses of the children by setting them an experimental task of travelling over the balance without touching it in any way. This led to the production of different shapes in the air, and travelling on body parts other than feet, so that different jumps, dive rolls and cartwheels were used.

Attention at this point was shifted from the mode of travelling used by the child when passing under, over and around his/her partner, to the shape that was being negotiated. Until this stage of development was reached, the shape had been essentially a static one, enabling safe, simple and varied negotiation. What would happen if the base shape moved slowly? Could a child pass over it safely in some way? This caused considerable excitement and many simple but original ideas were explored and executed.

With the exploration of a moving base shape, it became a natural progression for children to take the weight of their partners as they passed over them resulting in vaulting and sliding movements. Matching and contrasting shapes were then explored, e.g. one child first used a tucked jump to negotiate the curled shape of the barrier made by her partner. For contrast, she then used a stretched star jump to negotiate the obstacle again.

Each lesson in the gymnastics scheme included a section of work on the apparatus. In this section of the lesson the children were able to imagine the apparatus as part of a complete landscape, consisting of low and high points, inclines, or smooth or bumpy surfaces.

Initially, they passed over, under and around the apparatus in different ways individually. They then used the apparatus to make interesting shapes, producing a more varied and exciting landscape. Finally they moved around the apparatus in pairs with one child combining with the apparatus to enhance and add to the landscape, and make it more interesting for their partners to negotiate.

Since the children were to be working in pairs, and for a considerably large proportion of the scheme they were to be reliant upon each other, the teacher planned a tightly structured scheme in terms of stages of progressive development, but within the structure, gave opportunities for the children to use their imagination in creating and developing ideas.

Lesson plans for gymnastics _____

Holes and barriers

Cross-curricular projects

Lesson 1

Holes and barriers

Lesson 1

A Warm-up

1 'Can you run in and out of each other avoiding contact and stop when I give the signal?'

2 'Run in and out of each other and this time on a signal, stop in a bridge shape.'

3 'In pairs, one of you make the bridge shape and the other runs around the room passing under as many bridge shapes as possible.'

B Floorwork

1 'Remember the work we did, balancing on points and patches? Show me a balance and then run into a space and show me another, different one.'

2 'Decide on your favourite balance and make it perfect.'

3 'Show your balance to your partner and then both perform it, side-by-side matching. Change over.'

4 'Show me your favourite matched balance. A stay in the balance and B stand up and look at it. Is there anywhere you could wriggle under the balance or jump over it without touching the person? Change over.'

5 'Can A pass under and over your partner and then B pass under and over A. Can you join all those movements together smoothly?'

C Apparatus

1 'Let's explore the apparatus first by travelling over and under it.'

2 'Find a place on the apparatus where you can perform a good balanced position? Can you move on to another part of the apparatus and perform a different balance?'

3 'With your partner, one person finds a balanced position on or against the apparatus and the other one passes under or over it in some way? Don't forget to change over.'

D Calming-down activity

'Walk around the room side by side with your partner, keeping in step with him/her.'

Cross-curricular projects

Lesson 2

Holes and barriers

Lesson 2

A Warm-up

1 'Run in and out of each other and into spaces.'

2 'Can you run and jump to show different shapes in the air? In pairs, As crouch down as close to the floor as possible. Bs run in and out of As and jump over them when there is room to do so.

B Floorwork

1 'Remembering the balances from last lesson, can you think of a high-balanced position and a low-balanced position and then join them together smoothly?

2 'With your partner, watch each other's sequence and decide where you can go under or over your partner's balance.'

3 'Put your balances together in a sequence so that each partner negotiates the obstacles alternately.'

C Apparatus

1 'Explore the apparatus and remember how you can travel over and under it on your own.'

2 'On your own, travel on the floor and apparatus, and when possible stop and make a balanced position.'

3 'In pairs, one partner make a shape using the apparatus for the other one to pass over or under. Change over.'

D Calming-down activity

'Travel around the room sometimes close to the floor and sometimes far away from it.'

Cross-curricular projects

Lesson 3

Holes and barriers

Lesson 3

A Warm-up

1 'Move around the room on your hands and feet in different ways.'

2 'Run and jump into a space. When you land, sink down slowly into a long roll? Can you join those movements together?'

B Floorwork

1 'In your pairs, one partner lie flat on the floor with arms and legs outstretched. Can you travel over your partner without touching?

'Do you always have to jump? Could you use other parts of your body to take your weight?'

2 'What happens if the person lying down begins to roll slowly towards you? Can you still travel over them?'

3 'Are there any other ways the person on the floor can move slowly with their partner still travelling over them?'

4 'Join together two ideas where the obstacle is moving.'

C Apparatus

1 'Explore your apparatus, remembering to travel, under, over and around it.'

2 'Find places on your apparatus where you can long roll or slide.'

3 'Find ideas with a partner where one of you slides or long rolls and the other one crosses over.'

4 'Can you find two different ideas and join them together? Don't forget, you must take it in turns to cross over each other.'

D Calming-down activity

'Travel round the room following your partner. On a signal, the front one crouches low and the back one steps over to become the leader.'

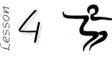

Cross-curricular projects

Lesson

4

Holes and barriers

Lesson 4

A Warm-up

1 'Run and jump to make different shapes in the air.'

2 'Travel in and out of each other on hands and feet in different ways.'

B Floorwork

1 'Remembering the long rolls we did last lesson – can you long roll over each other? When you do this, you are in contact with your partners. Can you find any other ways of crossing over your partner and being in contact with them?' Emphasise the need for a very stable base position.

2 'With your partner, make up a sequence to show movements going under and over each other with the base keeping still, and at least one movement when the base is moving.'

C Apparatus

1 'Explore your apparatus.'

2 'Being very careful and keeping your head up can you jump from low pieces of apparatus to show different shapes in the air?

3 'In twos, A makes a shape on or against the apparatus for B to travel over. Remember the different shapes you can make in the air?'

4 'One of you make a shape with or against the apparatus for the other one to travel over. This time you must have some contact with your partner.'

D Calming-down activity

'In a space, in "slow motion", keep changing your shape from low to high.'

Cross-curricular projects

Lesson

5

Holes and barriers

Lesson 5

A Warm-up

1 'Run and jump into the air showing really stretched shapes.'

2 'Can you now jump and show small, tucked shapes in the air? Remember to keep your head up at all times.'

B Floorwork

1 'In pairs, both show me a tucked shape on the floor. Try matching each other's shapes. Now show me a matching tucked jump in the air.'

2 'Show me how A makes a tucked shape on the floor with B doing a tucked jump over the top. Change over. Can you find any other matching or mirroring shapes with one partner on the floor and the other going over the top?'

3 'One of you curl up tightly on the floor and the other one stretch out as far as possible on the floor. Are these matching movements?' Establish with the children that these are contrasting movements.

'Can you show me different ideas where the obstacle and the person passing over or under are showing contrasting shapes?'

4 'Join together two sets of movements – one showing matching movements and the other showing contrasting ones.'

C Apparatus

1 'Explore your apparatus.'

2 'Experiment with your partner to produce matching or contrasting obstacles and travelling movements.'

3 'Put together two of these ideas.'

D Calming-down activity

'Move as slowly as possible around the room.'

Cross-curricular projects

Lesson **6**

Holes and barriers

Lesson 6

A Warm-up

1 'Run in and out of each other, and on a signal, stop in a space, crouched down. Do the same again, but stop in a bridge shape this time.'

2 'In pairs, one behind the other slowly trot or walk. When the front one comes to a space, make a shape for the one behind to pass over or under and then he/she becomes the new leader.'

B Floorwork

1 'Can you remember all the different ways of going over and under a partner?' Examples include hold a balance – go over or under; slowly moving base – go over or under; stable base – take weight to go over; matching or contrasting shapes go over or under.

'Make up a sequence showing four different ways of travelling over or under a partner. Take it in turns to be the shape, and have a good starting and finishing position.'

C Apparatus

1 'Explore your apparatus.'

2 'Remembering all the different ways of travelling over and under a partner and the apparatus, put together a sequence of four movements and a way of coming off the apparatus.'

D Calming-down activity

'Move round the room showing many different ways of travelling on hand and feet.'

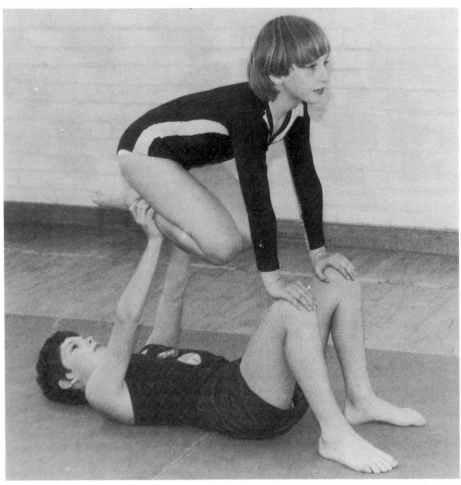

A stable base.

Counterbalance and countertension

The following work was produced as a direct result of looking at moving into a standing position from sitting on the ground!

How could so much work be initiated and evolve from one simple action?

The children were initially presented with the task of 'Sit on the floor, and without using your hands to help you, rise up to standing'. This produced a wide variety of answers, all of which were examined and analysed in terms of effort and the application of the specific forces of pushing and pulling.

Two examples of solving the problem included:

- sitting in a 'squat' position, twisting the knees to one side to move into the kneeling position before standing
- sitting in the 'squat' position, opening knees, drawing heels up close beneath the buttocks and pushing upwards and forwards to stand.

These examples clearly illustrated a strong pushing force exerted by the legs and an equally strong pulling force operating in the upper body, giving the necessary body tension and line to allow for standing.

To develop this idea further, it was necessary to narrow the boundaries of the task. The pupils were asked to sit in a squat position, keep their ankles and knees close together and stand up without hands touching the floor. This task proved altogether more taxing both physically and mentally. However, a small proportion of the class resolved the situation by rocking backwards and forwards several times before they used the resulting momentum to rise up into the standing position. This was an ingenious answer to the task, and one which everyone experienced before the task was limited to an even greater degree. Essentially, the task remained the same as the previous one, but no rocking or rolling was allowed.

The effort and physical strain this limited task produced was highly audible, and predictably the success rate was very low – indeed only one child, a very slender and supple girl managed to achieve the task successfully.

In the ensuing discussion on how the problem could be solved, i.e. standing up without hands touching the floor, the children decided it could be done by helping each other. The children found a partner and experimented with the idea. It worked – albeit generally in a very unsteady and unbalanced way. However, it was firmly established that pushing against the floor with the legs, while simultaneously pulling with the arms and upper part of the body allowed both partners to rise from the ground, and that it was imperative to have absolute trust in the reliability and co-operation of both participants in the action.

The children were then encouraged to look at several demonstrations, acknowledge the more successful ones in terms of keeping their balance, and to analyse critically why they were being more successful. These analyses helped the children to reach the conclusion that in order to maintain a balanced position throughout the action, and to remain in a balanced position in the final stages of the movement, still leaning away from each other, it was necessary to maintain a strong body tension, keep the arms straight and lean consistently away from each other. As they rose, they realised they should slowly straighten their bodies and not break the line by bending at the waist and sticking out their hips!

Much effort was involved in producing controlled, balanced movements, and the children learned, through sheer physical exertion, that body tension and the tension maintained between the two partners pulling away from each other were the critical teaching points of the skill. It, therefore, came as no surprise to learn that this type of movement was termed countertension.

Having thoroughly understood the forces required for successful countertension, the children were then encouraged to produce a countertension balance and then change the shape of it, by for example, slowly releasing the grip with one hand and both stretching away with that free hand to maintain the balance, but change its shape. Similarly, they were encouraged to produce balances by pulling or gripping different parts of their partners' bodies to create a countertension balance. This produced some very positive and creative work in pairs.

In the second gymnastics session, the knowledge and understanding gained by the class about countertension was applied, adapted and developed in the area of counterbalance.

After the warm-up and reminder of the work done in the previous lesson, the children were asked if there was any other way they could maintain a balanced position with a partner other than by pulling. Of course 'pushing' was an immediate collective response, whereupon the children developed, adapted and experimented with a large variety of creative ideas.

Attention to detail was encouraged in the children's observation and critical analysis of movement ideas, and through close questioning they discovered that there were many similarities between counterbalance and countertension, including the need for:

- absolute reliability and trust in a partner
- strong body tension
- equal pushing by both partners. This produces a balanced position which is interdependent.
  Differences in size and weight of partners will require adaptation of the force to be exerted.

These points were illustrated very clearly in one counterbalance movement in particular which was shown to the class and all children asked to attempt it. Partners sat back to back, with linked elbows, and heels pulled underneath the buttocks. Both sat with heads up, backs straight and pushed hard against the floor with their feet and hard against each others backs to push up to standing and remain in a balance pushing against one another.

Through experiment and discussion, the following definitions of counterbalance and countertension were reached:

- **Countertension** is achieved through gripping and pulling or leaning away from each other. The common base remains small, and a balanced position is felt when the body is subjected to forces acting in opposite directions, i.e. the pull of the partner through the gripping limbs and the pull of the rest of the body which leans away from both partner and base.
- **Counterbalance** is produced by pushing against or 'propping up' a partner and making adjustments in the area of their common base and in their angle of leaning, to achieve a position in which both are interdependent, each providing a force which balances and offsets the other.

Pushing and pulling work in the gymnastics lesson brought out many interesting points on the forces exerted, and the friction caused by body parts against each other or against the floor. These different points were examined and experimented with in science lessons.

It was established that friction is a force between two touching surfaces. When friction is low, for example between an ice skate and the ice, then sliding is easy. However, when friction is high, for example between a hand and a rope or between two hands in a secure grip, then sliding is difficult. This work naturally led into a discussion about the application of friction and its importance in road safety. Stopping distances for a car travelling at 15 metres per second (about 33 mph) were examined, and bar charts were constructed to show stopping distances for new and old tyres on wet and dry roads.

Occasionally, in the gymnastics lesson there was an obvious imbalance in size and weight of the two partners. This promoted a discussion on adjusting the pulling or pushing force in order to maintain a balanced position between the two people.

In science, this led to experimental work on the measurement of pushing and pulling forces using force meters. Once they had familiarised themselves with the force meters, the children then made predictions about the size of force (in Newtons) that was required to perform various actions, e.g. lifting a bag, pulling out a drawer, lifting an arm, pulling a chair across a room, lifting a table, pushing a table and pulling a table.

From these experiments there arose much speculation and discussion about the different jobs our muscles perform and how we use our muscles to move ourselves and other objects. The children tested the strength of finger and arm muscles by using bathroom scales measured in Newtons and indeed, also devised their own methods of muscle-force measurement.

In art and design technology lessons the concept of counterbalance was illustrated simply with the use of ruler and an object upon which to balance it. Working from this simple illustration, using wire or slender wooden strips and cardboard, the class was set the task of designing and producing a set of figures of different sizes and characters, all on the same theme, and constructing a well-balanced hanging mobile. This produced some beautifully worked and amazingly well-balanced butterfly, monster, family and hospital mobiles.

Reverting to the original simple stimulus of the ruler balanced on an object, it was discovered that the ruler could be set in motion by either an initiating push downwards or a pull upwards. Bearing this simple principle in mind, the object was to design and construct a simple projectile machine. The object to be projected was a pencil rubber, and an area of the classroom was designated as the test area. In this area, the children could, in turn, test fire their machines, at various stages of construction, from a certain spot on the floor towards a corner of the room.

Some incredibly ingenious machines were constructed and in one demonstration firing at the conclusion of the project, one small machine, much to the admiration of the rest of the class, fired the pencil rubber well over half-way across the classroom!

The following lesson plans illustrate the gymnastics work on counterbalance and countertension experienced by the class of 10–11-year-olds.

Work unit: Counterbalance/countertension

Aims of unit

To make a dance composition and gymnastics sequences incorporating work from other aspects of the curriculum.

Objectives	Lesson 1 Dance	Lesson 1 Gym	Lesson 2 Dance	Lesson 2 Gym	Lesson 3 Dance	Lesson 3 Gym	Lesson 4 Dance	Lesson 4 Gym	Lesson 5 Dance	Lesson 5 Gym	Lesson 6 Dance	Lesson 6 Gym	Lesson 7 Gym	Lesson 8 Gym
To enable the child to show, use and identify														
Concepts of counterbalance and countertension		[✓]		[✓]	[✓]	[✓]	[✓]	[✓]	✓	✓	✓	✓	✓	✓
To improve the child's performance, use and knowledge of														
a Canon and unison	✓	[✓]				✓			✓	✓	✓		✓	✓
b Pushing and pulling		[✓]	[✓]		✓	[✓]		[✓]		✓		[✓]	[✓]	[✓]
c Meeting and parting	✓	[✓]	✓			✓			✓	✓	✓	✓	✓	✓
d Making group shapes and formations								✓		[✓]	[✓]	✓	✓	✓
Through enlargement and the addition of basic actions enable the child to develop														
Mimetic movements into dance	[✓]		[✓]		✓				✓		✓			

Key: [✓] a main emphasis in the lesson   ✓ an emphasis in the lesson

All three aspects of each activity, i.e. composing, performing and appreciating in dance, and planning, performing and evaluating in gymnastics, should be apparent in every lesson.

Assessment

This should relate directly to the overall aims of the unit and the specific objectives for each lesson.

Dances within unit

Lessons 1–6   Waterless Method of Swimming Instruction

♪ *Accompaniment:*   No 13 on the cassette

Resources: *Waterless Method of Swimming Instruction* video, if available

Gymnastics within unit

Lessons 1–8   Counterbalance/countertension

Lesson plans for gymnastics ___

Counterbalance and countertension

Lesson 1

A Warm-up

1 'Can you run in and out of the mats, and when you come to a clear one, cross over it in some way?' Show some examples and establish whether the children are pushing or pulling against the floor and mats to cross over them. Through question and answer and experiencing the movement the children should notice that most of the actions require pushing from the floor and mats.

2 'Can you travel in and out of the mats by only pulling against the floor?' This task will be difficult and only a very small variety of pure pulling movements can be found.

B Floorwork

1 'Sit in a space, knees up in front of you, feet flat on the floor. Without opening knees, or using hands on the ground, how can you stand up?' The children will find that this requires quite considerable effort. Show some of the ideas and let the children try them out. Then explain how the task can be made much easier by working with a partner.

2 'Sit facing a partner, toes touching, knees drawn up, and gripping each others hands or wrists.' This will be done most successfully if the children are encouraged to:

   a pull and lean away from each other

   b maintain strong body tension

   c concentrate on their partner.

3 'Can you stand up and sit down with your partner in this position.' Teach the principle of pulling away from each other to maintain a balance and let the children experiment and establish it in their minds.

4 When the children can achieve this action successfully and in a balanced way, help them to develop the idea. 'Begin by sitting down, pull into a balance, then slowly release the grip of one hand and open out – still keeping the balance.'

5 Now open the task out to the children – 'Is there any other way you can pull against a partner in order to hold a balanced position?' Show examples of children gripping and pulling against different parts of each others' bodies.

6 Finish the lesson with a small sequence of movements. 'Can you start away from your mat and your partner, travel towards each other to hold a countertension position, and then travel away together.' Getting into the countertension position will need to be done slowly and carefully, while the movement away from each other could be explosive to act as a contrast.

C Calming-down activity

'Slide around the room using pushing/pulling movements.'

Cross-curricular projects

Lesson **2**

Counterbalance & countertension

Lesson 2

A Warm-up

1 Take out the mats and begin with a vigorous warm-up emphasising explosive movements – different jumps, fast rolls, round-offs, etc. As the children produce explosive movements, show some examples so all may see them and experience them if appropriate.

2 Recap the countertension sequence made with partners in the previous lesson. Remind the children of the teaching points.

B Floorwork

1 When the children have had a few minutes to practise their sequences see if they can produce a balance by pulling away from their partner. Encourage them to hold it for 3 seconds, and then explode away from each other. Show examples.

2 'We have established that by pulling against a partner we can hold a balanced position which cannot be achieved without each other. Is there any other way you can achieve a balanced position with a partner, other than by pulling?' The children should answer, 'Pushing'!

'Sit down back to back with a partner. Link your elbows and tense your body, tuck your heels up close to your bottom and keeping your head up and back straight, push hard against your partner's back and hard with your feet against the floor to stand up, still leaning against each other.'

3 'This time to prove you have the correct push, can you do it without linking elbows?'

4 Now redefine the task and ask the children if there are any other ways to push against partners to hold a balanced position? Allow time for experimentation and then choose some examples to show the class, allowing the children to try some ideas other than their own.

Finish the lesson with a short sequence: 'Start away from the mat and your partner – travel towards each other quickly, hold a balanced position by pushing against your partner and then travel away together, slowly.' Encourage the children to use different directions and levels in their sequence.

C Calming-down activity

'Show different ways of holding a balanced position on the floor by pushing against it.'

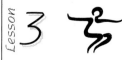

Cross-curricular projects

Lesson **3**

Counterbalance & countertension

Lesson 3

A Warm-up

1 'Travel in and out of the benches and mats, and when a bench is free, travel over it or under it in different ways.' Show some examples and establish whether the child is pushing or pulling against the apparatus to produce the movement.

2 'Can you travel round the room:
   a pushing from feet?
   b pushing from hands?
   c pulling along the bench with different parts of the body facing the bench?'

At this point it would be expedient to do some work on jumping from the bench, using it as a take-off board. Can the children produce different shapes in the air and do they take off from one foot or two feet?

B Small apparatus

1 'Having practised freely, go back to your own bench. You remember the movements we were doing during the last two lessons – pushing or pulling against your partner to hold a balanced position. Can you now push or pull against your partner and the apparatus in order to hold a balanced position?' Allow the children to experiment and then show some examples so they may try ideas other than their own.

C Apparatus

1 'Explore your own apparatus – over/under/around. Use mats and the floor.'

2 'Travel around your apparatus taking weight on different parts of your body – are you pushing or pulling in order to travel over the apparatus?' Show some examples and establish whether each involves pushing or pulling. Give time for the children to experiment with some of these ideas.

Then set a specific task – 'Can you push away from your apparatus using your hands/feet?' It is important to change apparatus frequently during these tasks.

D Calming-down activity

'Hold a balanced position showing firm body tension. On a signal, relax and "melt" down on to the floor.'

Cross-curricular projects
Lesson **4**
Counterbalance & countertension

Lesson 4

A Warm-up

Take mats and benches out and use them to show pushing/pulling on different body parts.

B Small apparatus

1 'Move on to your own bench and experiment with different balances, using pushing and pulling.' Show some examples.

2 'By yourself can you now join together three balances? Somewhere in the sequence there must be an explosive movement.'

C Apparatus

1 'Take out your own apparatus and explore it.'

2 'Travel between all the apparatus, and when you come to a clear piece, push or pull against it in order to hold a balanced position. Hold each balance for 3 seconds before moving out of it and into another balance.' Remind the children of the need for strong body tension to achieve good balances.

3 Demonstrations should be shown to give the children ideas and to reinforce the teaching points.

D Calming-down activity

'Moving continuously, balance and "melt", balance and "melt", etc.'

Lesson 5

A Warm-up

1 'Run anywhere in the room and when I clap my hands, jump as high as possible.' Repeat several times.

2 'Run anywhere in the room, and when I clap my hands, hold a balanced position on the floor. Remember to push against the floor, keep your body tense and stretch parts of the body not bearing weight.'

B Apparatus

1 'Take out the same set of apparatus you had last lesson. Using all the apparatus in the hall, travel in and out of it, and when you come to a free piece, hold a balanced position against it or on it by pulling or pushing. Hold the balance for 3 seconds and then move to another piece of apparatus and another balance.' Show some examples.

2 'Go back to your own piece of apparatus and with a partner, pull or push against your partner *and* the apparatus in order to hold a balanced position.'

3 Experiment with the ideas and show examples on each different type of apparatus – establish whether the balance is counterbalance or countertension.

4 'Can you travel towards the apparatus and your partner and hold your balance on the apparatus?' Discuss the use of different directions and speeds.

5 'Show demonstrations of several ideas and then set the task of travelling towards the apparatus, holding the balance with your partner and then travelling away again.'

C Calming-down activity

'Trot around the room avoiding contact with anyone else – gradually slow down until you stop.'

Lesson 6

A Warm-up

Begin with a vigorous warm-up on the floor. Use anything done in previous lessons.

B Apparatus warm-up

1 'Run in and out of the apparatus not touching it at all.'

2 'Run in and out of the apparatus, and under any clear pieces.'

3 'Run in and out of the apparatus, and when you come to a clear piece go over it, or under it.' You should n*ever* include the ropes in this type of warm-up.

C Apparatus

1 'Go to your own piece of apparatus and practise the sequence you made with your partner last lesson.'

2 'Change apparatus. Experiment with other ideas using counterbalance/countertension.' Show examples of ideas and change apparatus again.

3 'Compose a sequence. Join together *three* counterbalance/countertension movements, one of which must be on the mats. You must also include variations in speed, direction and levels.'

D Calming-down activity

'Follow my leader with your partner – reacting to changes of speed, direction and level.'

Cross-curricular projects

Lessons

7-8

Waterless swimming

Lessons 7 and 8

A Warm-up

1 'Travel in and out of all the apparatus. Stop.' Repeat several times.

2 'Run in/out of the apparatus and when I call out "Stop", you pull or push against the nearest piece of apparatus or the floor to hold a balance – then move on.' Repeat several times.

3 'Run in/out of the apparatus, and when I call out "Stop" make as small a shape as possible against or on the apparatus.' Repeat several times.

4 'Do the same thing, but when you have held the ball/small shape for a count of three, explode out/and move on to another piece and repeat – all in your own time.'

5 'Run in/out of the apparatus, and when I call out "Stop" shake hands with the person closest to you and lean away – then move on.' Repeat several times.

Several of these warm-ups may be used for each lesson.

B Apparatus

1 'Move on to your own piece of apparatus and remember your sequence from last week.'

Remember, in your distribution of children you will have approximately two groups of two to each small set of apparatus, therefore, you can now ask them to work together in a four.

2 'Can you find a group balance where everyone is pushing or pulling against their partners and/or the apparatus to hold a balanced position?' Give them time to experiment and look at some ideas.

A group balance.

3 'Can you start away from the apparatus and move into the balance neatly.'

4 'Can you find a way of moving out of the balance – remember you could "explode".'

5 The finished sequence should be – move into the balance/balance/move ('explode') away. Change apparatus when you have seen the sequence.

C Calming-down activity

'Work out a series of steps and runs which you can repeat and travel round the room.'

Dance

The initial stimulus for the dance work was the video recording of *Waterless Method of Swimming Instruction*. The dance was choreographed by Robert Cohan for London Contemporary Dance Theatre and is set in an empty swimming pool on board a cruise liner.

As emphasised in Chapter 1 it is vital that pupils should have access to professional dance models and *Waterless Method of Swimming Instruction* is a particularly relevant model for children with little or no dance experience. It is easily understood and shows very clearly the use of many choreographic devices. It is divided into fairly short sections and most of these could be used as a starting point for dance composition. While many of the sections can stand alone, it must be emphasised, however, that at some time during the children's work they should see the whole dance as it was intended to be seen by the choreographer.

The section used for this particular project is approximately 2 minutes into the video and begins with two male dancers sliding into the empty swimming pool. The dancers then perform a duo based on the idea of diving and supporting each other in the water.

Before the children were shown this section of the video they were asked to consider the following:

1 What are the two main dancers actually doing?
2 How do their movements differ from reality?
3 How do the dancers work with each other?

The answer to the first question is relatively obvious in that the dancers appear to be diving and they then support each other as if helping each other to swim.

While the second question appears to be more difficult, it was answered with surprising ease. Perhaps the most important point was that jumps were used instead of head-first dives. It was also established that a variety of arm and leg gestures, not always associated with diving were used in the execution of the jumps. Other observations included the fact that sideways jumps were performed as well as forwards and backwards jumps, which are directions more associated with diving, and that the steps, bounces and jumps used in the diving section were patterned and made into phrases which were repeated.

The third question posed little difficulty, with the pupils noting that at the beginning of the extract the two dancers were doing the same movements at the same time, both facing in the same direction, one slightly behind the other. They then jumped away from each other before meeting again to support each other.

These observations gave us ample material from which we could make our own dance. We then watched the video extract once more before deciding on our own dance framework. The children were initially only shown the extract twice, so that they did not attempt to copy the detail of the dance, but instead used it as a stimulus for their own composition.

We decided to use the two ideas of diving and supporting each other in the water as our initial starting point just as had been used in the video. Each pupil was encouraged to experiment with the five basic jumps, adding their own arm and leg gestures. They then made their own patterns of steps, bounces and jumps before beginning to work with a partner. It was at first decided that the basis for the 'diving' partner sequence would be working in unison, with meeting and parting. The section was later extended to include the use of canon and unison.

It was left to the pupils whether they used both of their individual 'diving' sequences and taught them to each other in their entirety or whether they used part of each other's sequences to create a third sequence.

Initially, the accompaniment used for this section came from the video extract itself, with the monitor being turned away from the children as the video was playing. Eventually, the dance was performed in a local theatre as part of a dance evening and music was then composed especially for the dance composition.

Once the 'diving' section of the dance was completed the pupils began to work on the section of the dance in which the dancers supported each other. In the video extract only one method of support was used and this was repeated four times. It was at this point that the pupils' work on counterbalance and countertension in gymnastics came into its own. Various ways of supporting someone in the water were discussed, as were the different relationships which could be used.

From this discussion and experimentation with ideas, it was decided that at least four methods of support using both counterbalance and countertension should be used. It was also established that a variety of levels would make the sequence more visually interesting.

Many different ways of supporting each other were tried, but it was important that they conveyed the intended idea of the dance, rather than merely replicating feats tried in gymnastics lessons. Much emphasis was therefore placed on the different ways that people are supported in the water, either when they are learning to swim or during life-saving practices. Pupils tried supporting each other, for example, by holding their partner's head, under their middles or in the small of their back. Having experimented with the ideas, they were then translated into counterbalance or countertension as described in the gymnastics unit on pages 161–6.

Once the static positions were selected and practised, it was then necessary to devise the most appropriate ways of linking the sequence together, but all the time bearing in mind the swimming and diving idea. Some of the jumps from the 'diving' sequence were used, as were dive forward rolls. Some pupils launched themselves to slide in a gliding movement along the ground, while their partners jumped over them. Others used arm gestures based on swimming strokes to initiate turns to take them into the next position with their partner.

By this time a great deal of material had been generated and it was decided that a whole class dance could be choreographed and the following form was eventually agreed. The dancers would begin on the opposite side of the 'stage' from their partner. One of the pair would enter with his/her own 'diving' sequence. Once everyone had finished their sequence the rest of the dancers would enter with his/her 'diving' sequence and finish next to his/her partner. The pair would then dance their joint 'diving' sequence in unison, leading directly into the counterbalance/countertension sequence. The dance finished with the dancers performing their original 'diving' sequence in canon to take them off-stage.

It was at this point that some pupils mentioned the other dancers they had seen at the beginning of the video extract. These had been standing at the back of the pool while the two main dancers had entered it. It was agreed that this idea could be incorporated into the class's dance. Four groups of six or seven pupils got together to form a tableau depicting a seaside scene. These ranged from surfing and water-skiing to sunbathing and paddling to eating ice-cream or watching Punch and Judy. Each group had to depict two tableaux or photographs and find smooth transitions from one to the other.

Some of the considerations already mentioned earlier in the chapter were taken into account when the group 'photographs' were being formed in order to make them as visually interesting as possible. Questions were asked, for example, about level, focus, relationship and spacing, helping the children to clarify their ideas and to make their intentions clear in visual terms.

Instead of starting off-stage, the dancers now began in their group 'photographs', and it was to the same 'photographs' that they returned at the end of the dance.

The following is a suggested dance framework and a unit of work. As stated previously, these are only suggestions and should be adapted to suit particular children and situations.

Lesson plans for dance

Waterless method of swimming instruction

Dance framework

1 Groups of six or seven children in seaside 'photograph'. Hold for six counts, then slowly and smoothly form a second 'photograph' and hold for six counts.

2 As dance their individual diving sequence.

3 Bs dance their sequence to meet their partners.

4 As and Bs dance their combined diving sequence.

5 Duo sequence based on counterbalance/countertension.

6 As and Bs dance their diving sequence to finish in the first group photographs.

Lesson 1

Cross-curricular projects

Lesson 1

Waterless swimming

Introduce the dance idea by giving some background information about the dance. This can be found on the video in an interview with Robert Cohan immediately prior to the dance.

Give out the questions (see page 166) and watch the relevant video extract. Discuss the answers with the class and show the extract again.

The whole of the above should take approximately 6–7 minutes.

A Introduction

Anything involving the small bounces seen on the video, travelling from space to space, e.g.

8 small bounces
8 small steps
Repeat
Stretch into a star shape (4 counts)
Close the body into a compact shape (2 counts)
Repeat the whole sequence.

Any accompaniment with regular counts can be used.

B Movement exploration and development

1 'Show me a two-feet to two-feet jump. Show me again and think about the position of your arms in the air at the height of the jump. What would they look like if you were diving? Think about the position of your legs. Are they tucked up underneath you or are they straight? If they are tucked up, remember not to drop your head down to meet them.'

2 'Show me a short run as a preparation for your jump. How many steps did you take? Can you repeat the run and jump and make it exactly the same each time? Find a partner, ask them how many steps they take and then look at that phrase

and see if they are right.' This gives the children time to catch their breath, encourages their observational skills, as well as helping them to refine their own performance.

3 'Go back into your own space and let's quickly recap the five basic jumps. Choose at least two different jumps and join them together with running steps. Remember to think about the position of your arms and legs in the air. Remember, too, that you can jump backwards and sideways as well as forwards.'

4 'Working in pairs, check that your partner is using at least two different jumps. Can you help him/her with the position of their arms and legs in the air?

5 'Go back into your own space. You remember the small bounces that you saw on the video as if the dancers were testing the springboard. Make a pattern using no more than eight bounces to include in your own sequence.' Encourage variety, e.g. bounces close to the floor, small and larger bounces, bounces in different directions.

6 'Decide where you are going to include the bouncing pattern in your running and jumping sequence. You may use it as many times as you like. Sometimes you may only use part of it if you wish.'

C Dance

Practise the sequence made so far.

D Calming-down activity

Any relaxation exercise on the floor.

Cross-curricular projects

Lesson 2

Waterless swimming

Lesson 2

A Introduction

'Practise the sequence you made in the last lesson.'

B Movement exploration and development

1 'Find a partner and show each other your sequence.'

2 'Teach each other your sequence.'

3 'With the material you have, make a combined sequence. You may decide to do both sequences or you may decide to take elements from each of your sequences to make a new one.' Encourage the use of different relationships, e.g. partners one behind the other or beside each other or facing each other.

Also encourage

a meeting and parting

b leading and following

c the use of canon and unison.

C Dance

1 'The space you are working in now is the space in which you will always meet your partner. Decide who will be A and who will be B in your partnership. Go "off-stage" on the opposite side from your partner.'

2 'All As dance your diving sequence.'

3 'All Bs dance your sequence. Make sure that you finish in the correct space to begin the combined sequence with your partner.'

4 'Dance your combined sequence.'

5 Dance 2–4 of the framework.

D Calming-down activity

Any relaxation exercise.

Cross-curricular projects

Lesson **3**

Waterless swimming

Lesson 3

A Introduction

Repeat the warm-up sequence learned in Lesson 1.

B Movement exploration and development

1 'How can you support someone in the water?' You could demonstrate with a pupil some of the suggestions made.

2 'With your partner, experiment with some of these ideas.' Make sure that it is not always the same person supporting or being supported.

3 'How can we make this section of the dance more exciting?' Remind them of the work previously done in gymnastics lessons on counterbalance and countertension. 'Decide which of your supports could best be counterbalance and which could be countertension.' Remind them of the teaching points for countertension, i.e.

   a pulling away from each other

   b body tension

   c concentration upon their partner

   and for counterbalance – pushing towards their partner again with body tension and concentration upon their partner.

4 Allow time for experimentation and then look at some examples to see why pairs are being successful and also to show the variety of ideas being used.

C Dance

'Let's finish by practising your individual diving sequence and the combined sequence you made with your partner last lesson', i.e. 2–4 of the framework.

D Conclusion

Any relaxation exercise.

Cross-curricular projects

Lesson **4**

Waterless swimming

Lesson 4

A Introduction

Repeat the warm-up sequence learned in Lesson 1.

B Movement exploration and development

1 'Practise the counterbalance and countertension sequences that you made with

your partner in the last lesson.' Encourage the use of different relationships with their partner, e.g. facing, back to back, side by side, above and below.

2 'Choose at least four examples of counterbalance and countertension. Experiment with the transitions between them.'

Through discussion and experimentation encourage movements such as lowering their partners, spinning their partners, diving underneath or over the top of them. Jumps from their diving sequences could also be used. It is vital, however, constantly to remind children of the dance idea of supporting their partner in the water, so that this section of the dance does not look like a gymnastics sequence.

C Dance

1 Recap the individual and combined diving phrases.

2 Dance the diving section, followed by the counterbalance/countertension section, i.e. 2–5 of the framework.

D Conclusion

Any relaxation exercise.

Lesson 5

A Introduction

Anything involving stretching, travelling and jumping.

The rest of the lesson should be used to recap the sections of the dance already learned, putting them together, practising them and viewing the results.

Lesson 6

A Introduction

Anything involving stretching, travelling and jumping.

B Dance

Practise the dance learned so far.

C Movement exploration and development

Look at the video extract again with particular reference to the spectators by the pool. Discuss what makes their groupings effective. Discuss what activities you might expect to find by the side of a pool or at the seaside.

1 'In groups of six or seven, make yourselves into a seaside or poolside photograph. One member of the group can stand outside as the photographer to act as the group choreographer.' Make sure that each member of the group has a turn to do this.

2 'Choose two of the group's favourite photographs and experiment with transitions between the two. Decide which will be your first group photograph. Hold it for a count of six before moving smoothly and slowly with as little travelling as possible into the second group photograph.' Practise this.

D Dance

Practise the whole dance as described in the framework. Video it if possible.

E Conclusion

Discuss and evaluate the dance.

6 Useful Addresses

Arts Council of Great Britain
Dance Department
14 Great Peter Street
London SW14 3NQ
- *Provides information.*

Council for Dance Education and Training
5 Tavistock Place
London WC1H 9SS
- *Provides information.*

Dance Books Ltd
9 Cecil Court
London WC2N 4EZ
- *Supplies books, videos, music cassettes.*

Dance and the Child International
Dance Department
Froebel College
Roehampton Institute
Roehampton Lane
London SW15 5PH
- *Provides periodicals, courses/conferences, information.*

English Folk Dance and Song Society
2 Regents Park Road
London NW1 7AY
- *Provides periodicals, courses/conferences, information; supplies books, music cassettes.*

National Association of Teachers in Further and Higher Education
Dance Section
Hamilton House,
Mabledon Place
London WC1H 9BH
- *Provides periodicals, courses/conferences, information.*

National Dance Teachers Association
Marion Wallace
5 Dunvegan Way
Putnoe Lane
Bedford MK41 8PE
- *Provides periodicals, courses/conferences, information.*

National Resource Centre for Dance
University of Surrey
Guildford
Surrey GU2 5XH
- *Provides periodicals, courses/conferences, information; supplies videos.*

The Physical Education Association of Great Britain and Northern Ireland
Ling House
5 Western Court
Bromley Street
Birmingham B9 4AN
- *Provides periodicals, courses/conferences, information.*

Standing Conference on Dance in Higher Education
c/o Department of Dance Studies
University of Surrey
Guildford
Surrey GU2 5XH
- *Provides periodicals, courses/conferences, information.*

Philip Taylor
55 Gardner Street
Glasgow G11 5D
- *Supplies music cassettes.*

Val Sabin Publications
1 King Edward Road
Northampton NN1 5LY
- *Supplies Key Stage 1 and Key Stage 2 teaching manuals for gymnastics.*

Appendix: Bodywork As A Resource for Scottish Primary Teachers

Bodywork supplies Scottish primary teachers with resource material for the implementation of many aspects of the Physical Education component in the *Expressive Arts 5–14: Curriculum and Assessment in Scotland National Guidelines* (Scottish Office Education Department, HMSO, 1992).

In Scotland an over-arching policy statement in Physical Education, which would include dance and gymnastics, is the norm.

The end of Key Stage descriptions align sympathetically with the attainment targets across the levels A–E. These attainment targets are viewed as milestones to be passed rather than barriers to be surmounted. The programmes of study illustrated articulate well with the attainment outcome 'Expressing feeling, ideas, thoughts and solutions' outlined within the Physical Education section of the *Expressive Arts* document and in particular the strand 'Creating and designing'.

The following co-relation chart ties attainment targets to Key Stages.

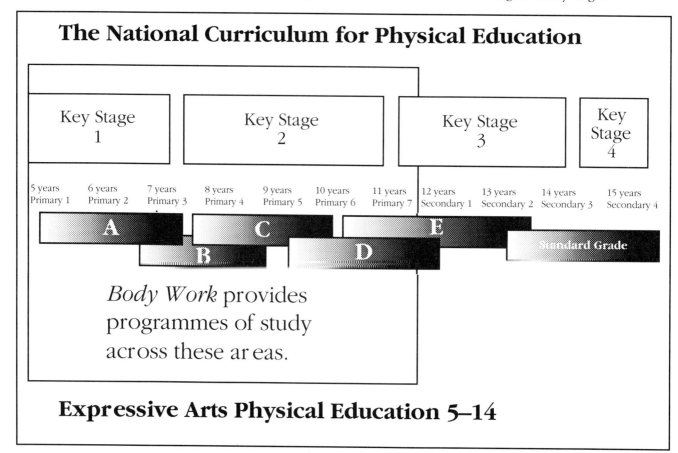

The National Curriculum for Physical Education

| Key Stage 1 | Key Stage 2 | Key Stage 3 | Key Stage 4 |

| 5 years Primary 1 | 6 years Primary 2 | 7 years Primary 3 | 8 years Primary 4 | 9 years Primary 5 | 10 years Primary 6 | 11 years Primary 7 | 12 years Secondary 1 | 13 years Secondary 2 | 14 years Secondary 3 | 15 years Secondary 4 |

A   B   C   D   E   Standard Grade

Body Work provides programmes of study across these areas.

Expressive Arts Physical Education 5–14

The following table links the good practice suggested in *Bodywork* to the *Expressive Arts 5–14*. Teachers are referred to the relevant page numbers in both.

Bodywork

Expressive Arts 5–14

page 9 – Developing schemes of work:

1 Undertake an analysis of resources to include staff expertise and available equipment.

2 Undertake a time analysis to establish how much time will be committed to teaching dance and gymnastics across the Key Stage.

3 Allocate time, term by term across each of the years in the Key Stage.

4 Read Key Stages.

page 55 – Decisions regarding the development of appropriate programmes of study should be guided by current good practice, resources and the notion of a balanced curriculum.

page 10 – Much of the detail of individual programmes and their implementation will differ from school to school, according to the needs and interests of pupils and the school's priorities and circumstances.

pages 60–72 – For Key Stage, refer to level of attainment.

page 10 – By end of Key Stage 1, pupils should be able to:

a plan and perform safely a range of simple actions and linked movements in response to given tasks and stimuli

b practise and improve their performance

c describe what they and others are doing

page 58 – Attainment target: Level A

• **Creating and designing:** select and organise appropriate responses to given tasks

• **Co-operating, sharing, communicating and competing:** show their movement ideas to others and respond to simple movement signals given by others

• **Using the body:** perform a range of single actions, such as running, stretching and balancing with some control of body weight

• **Observing, reflecting, describing and responding:** observe simple actions, describe some features of these and offer some personal response at a simple level

page 11 – By end of Key Stage 1, pupils should be able to:

a plan, practise, improve and remember more complex sequences of movement

b practise and improve their performance

c describe what they and others are doing

page 58 – Attainment target: Level A

• **Creating and designing:** select and organise appropriate responses to simple given tasks

• **Co-operating, sharing, communicating and competing:** show their movement ideas to others and respond to simple movement signals given by others

• **Using the body:** perform a range of simple actions, such as running, stretching and balancing with some control of body weight

• **Observing, reflecting, describing and responding:** observe simple actions, describe some features of these and offer some personal response at a simple level

page 11 – By end of Key Stage 1, pupils should be able to:

page 59 – Attainment target: Level A

a plan, practise, improve and remember more complex sequences of movement

b perform effectively in activities requiring quick decision making

c respond safely, alone and with others, to challenging tasks, taking account of levels of skill and understanding

d evaluate how they and others perform and behave against criteria suggested by the teacher and suggest ways of improving their performance

pages 14–17 – Assessment

page 18 – By end of Key Stage 1, pupils should be able to:

a plan and perform safely a range of simple actions and linked movements in response to given tasks and stimuli

- **Creating and designing:** express ideas and feelings through more complex sequences of movements

- **Applying skills:** use knowledge and understanding to apply skills with control and accuracy in predictable situations, e.g. a dance or a game

- **Creating and designing:** demonstrate a range of responses to structured tasks

- **Observing, reflecting, describing and responding:** observe, reflect upon and describe performance of self and peers, against specific given criteria; offer evaluative comment and suggest ways of improving skills

The content of this section of the book relates well to emphasis of *Expressive Arts 5–14*. For further information, refer to *Curriculum and Assessment in Scotland: A Policy for the 90s* (HMSO, 1987).

Attainment target: Level A

page 62 –

- **Using the body:** the choice of equipment, apparatus and environments should be sufficiently broad and balanced to allow pupils to extend their basic movement experience.

  Teachers should introduce pupils to handling small equipment: orderly retrieval and replacement; using space safely and effectively

page 64 –

- **Applying skills:** tasks should require pupils to perform actions which focus on one quality or contrast the qualities, e.g. a slow bend followed by a fast stretch, travelling with a change of strength from strong to light, kicking with force or lightness

page 66 –

- **Creating and designing:** teachers should provide opportunities for pupils to use their bodies to respond to simple tasks on the floor and on apparatus; to respond to ideas, thoughts and feelings; to show moods; to portray characters or events to tell stories, real or imaginary

b practise and improve their performance

page 64 –

- **Applying skills:** multiple and varied opportunities should be given so that pupils can practise and improve their ability to perform the basic actions in a range of simple contexts, e.g. jumping and landing in gymnastics, dance, games and athletics

page 68 –

- **Co-operating, sharing, communicating and competing:** teachers should organise opportunities for pupils to work co-operatively together in terms of the tasks set and in the use of space, sharing of apparatus, exchanging of equipment with others, etc.

page 18 –

c describe what they and others are doing

page 70 –

- **Evaluating and appreciating:** opportunities should be provided for the pupils to watch each others' work and for asking them to describe specific content, e.g. 'In what direction did Mary move?'

d recognise the effects of physical activities on their bodies

page 60 –

- **Investigating and developing fitness:** pupils should be encouraged to discuss how they feel after such activity and describe what happens to the body, such as feeling hot and tired

page 19 – By end of Key Stage 2, pupils should be able to:

Attainment target: Level C

a plan, practise, improve and remember more complex sequences of movement

c i respond safely to challenging tasks alone

page 63 –

- **Using the body:** to help them improve fluency and control, pupils should be encouraged to explore ways of linking movement patterns and skills and to experiment with changes in force and speed and with timing, e.g. experimenting with twisting and turning to change direction smoothly; learning to control the pace of the ball in redirecting a pass

c respond safely, alone and with others to challenging tasks, taking account of levels of skill and understanding

page 69 –

- **Co-operating, sharing, communicating and competing:** pupils should be encouraged and given the opportunity to work together co-operatively in exploring ideas and tackling tasks

e evaluate how well they and others perform and behave against criteria suggested by the teacher

Gourlay Jenkins and Grant Blair
Staff Tutors of Physical Education, Fife Region